art / shop / eat
PARIS

Delia Gray-Durant

Louvre Tuileries

The Louvre **6**
on route 44
commercial galleries 47
eating and drinking 47
shopping 52

Beaubourg Marais

Centre Pompidou **60**
Musée Picasso **76**
on route 80
commercial galleries 82
eating and drinking 83
shopping 88

Left Bank St-Michel

Musée du Moyen Age **96**
on route 103
commercial galleries 105
eating and drinking 106
shopping 111

D'Orsay St-Germain

Musée d'Orsay **116**
Musée Rodin **129**
on route 133
commercial galleries 135
eating and drinking 136
shopping 140

entertainment 147

planning 153

art glossary 172

maps 185

introduction

The magnetism of Paris is so irresistible that it is impossible not to be seduced by its many charms. The wealth of the city's historic culture expressed in the sheer splendour of its public monuments and the magnificence of its art collections, awe and amaze, while at the leading edge of art, architecture and design, *haute couture* and gastronomy, Paris is second to none.

In order to guide you through the vast choice of artistic, eating and shopping opportunities in Paris, this book is arranged into four art districts focussing on six major collections. On the Right Bank of the Seine are the Musée du Louvre, and the Centre Pompidou and Musée Picasso; on the Left Bank, the Musée du Moyen Age, and the Musée d'Orsay and Musée Rodin. There is also information on many other museums and monuments, as well as the commercial art galleries to be found in these art areas.

Each of the four districts, or *quartiers*, has its particular personality which becomes apparent in the sections devoted to eating and shopping. The elegant designer boutiques and restaurants between the Louvre and the Champs-Elysées contrast with the more trendy area around the Pompidou Centre and the Picasso Museum. Across the river, the Museum of the Middle Ages is at the heart of the student district, where cheap eateries vie with some of the best restaurants in Paris. Neighbouring St-Germain, around the Musée d'Orsay and Musée Rodin, is heaven for shoppers of all ages, offering everything from contemporary fashion to antiques as well as a wide variety of cuisine.

The planning section will help with practical details before and during your trip, while entertainment suggests activities ranging from classical concerts to funky night clubs. Finally, there's an art glossary with essential background on leading artists and personalities connected with Paris. *Bon voyage et bon appétit.*

LOUVRE
TUILERIES

Musée du Louvre

OPEN	Wed–Sun 9.00–18.00; Mon, certain galleries until 21.45; Wed, most galleries open until 21.45; History of the Louvre, Mon 9.00–18.00; Medieval Louvre same hours as museum
CLOSED	Tues, 1/1, 1/5, 14/7, 25/12
CHARGES	€7.50 before 15.00, €5 after 15.00 and all day Sunday. Admission free, on presentation of valid proof of eligibility, for under 18s; art, archaeology and architecture students; recipients of certain social benefits (unemployed); teachers and researchers in an educational establishment; school and student groups accompanied by a teacher; disabled visitors and their carers. Admission free for all on first Sun of the month and on 14 July
TELEPHONE	**01 40 20 50 50**; or **01 40 20 51 51** (recorded); events **01 40 20 55 55** (recorded), or **01 01 40 20 67 89** information **01 40 20 53 17**
WWW.	**louvre.fr**
MAIN ENTRANCE	Pyramid, Cour Napoléon. **Other entrances**: Porte des Lions, 9.00–17.30 (closed Fri), Carrousel du Louvre. Ticket holders only from Passage Richelieu
METRO	Palais-Royal-Musée du Louvre, Louvre-Rivoli, Tuileries
DISABLED ACCESS	The museum is well adapted to disabled visitors with a lift inside the Pyramid, and lifts and ramps throughout the buildings. Wheelchairs can be loaned and there is an orientation guide in English and French. **T 01 40 20 59 90**
PUBLICATIONS	As well as the free plan of the Louvre, booklets, pamphlets, guides and monographs are on sale in each wing. Most galleries contain broadsheets in several languages with information on exhibits. Wall panels give the history of certain rooms. *Louvre guide de visite*, F. Bayle, €8, available in English; *Les Nocturnes du lundi*; free, French only
AUDIO GUIDES	Available in English in each of the three museum wings, €5
PHOTOGRAPHY	Hand-held cameras may be used but no flash or tripods
CYBER LOUVRE	Multimedia resource for the Louvre, Wed–Mon 10.00–18.45, **T 01 40 20 67 30**
SHOPS	Between Hall Napoléon and the Carrousel du Louvre are a large bookshop, boutiques selling reproductions, prints, posters and postcards. The Chalcographie du Musée sells prints, some made from original plates. There is also a post office. (All open to non-ticket holders)

EATING   Non-ticket holders: **Restaurant du Grande Louvre** (reasonably-priced set menus); **Café du Louvre**, in Halle Napoléon. Ticket-holders only: **Café Mollien**, 1st floor, Denon wing, and **Café Denon**, lower ground floor (light meals); **Café Richelieu**, 1st floor, Richelieu wing (snacks and light meals)

The Louvre is also the venue for frequent temporary exhibitions, lectures, films and concerts.

Magnificent and immense, the Musée du Louvre is one of the world's most famous and diverse museums. It consists of seven departments (see below) divided between three main wings, Richelieu (north), Sully (east) and Denon (south), each on four levels. The oldest part of the building, described as the Medieval Louvre, is the Lower Ground Floor of Sully Wing.

The extent of the building and the collections can be daunting and the best way to take on the Louvre is to decide whether to go for a department, a wing, or certain highlights. To help in this, the section on the Collections is arranged by department and as far as possible by wing. Painting and Sculpture are mainly in Richelieu and partly in Denon, and each is sub-divided by country. Oriental (Middle Eastern) Antiquities and Objets d'Art are in Richelieu and Sully. Egyptian Antiquities and Greek, Etruscan and Roman Antiquities are mainly in Sully with a small part in Denon. Drawings is linked to Paintings. On temporary loan is a small display of African, Asian, Oceanic and early American Arts in Denon. Be sure to check which galleries are closed on certain days (information available in the reception area). Suggested highlights are indicated for each collection.

The main reception area under the Pyramid, Hall Napoléon, is below ground, and from here escalators (and lifts) ascend to the lower ground floor of each wing.

THE BUILDING

The Palais du Louvre stands between Rue de Rivoli and the River Seine and despite its apparent homogeneity, it is the result of many phases of building. The Old Louvre consisted of the royal palace surrounding the Cour Carrée to the east, and the long

Pavillon de Sully and Pyramide du Louvre

gallery along the banks of the Seine. The site was first earmarked by Philippe Auguste for a fortress (1190-1202), which was transformed by Charles V (1364-80) into an official royal residence. Subsequent monarchs preferred other palaces until, during the 16c, François I, Charles IX and Henri IV carried out grand schemes at the Louvre, while the Palais des Tuileries to the west was begun for Catherine de Medicis in 1564. With contributions from Louis XIII and Louis XIV, by 1661 the Cour Carrée had taken its present form. When Louis XIV turned his attention to his new palace at Versailles and abandoned Paris, the Louvre took on a new role as home to the academies including, in 1692, an Academy of Painting and Sculpture, which held exhibitions of members' works twice a year. The fabric of the palace was, however, neglected and continued to deteriorate until a powerful public lobby convinced Louis XV to begin restoring the site in 1754. Gradually, during the reign of Louis XVI (1774-93), despite financial and practical difficulties, the project for a French museum began to take shape.

The scheme was accelerated following the Revolution, and in 1793 the Musée de la République opened in the Louvre. Enriched by the acquisition of collections formerly belonging to royalty, to emigrants and to the Church, its role gradually evolved from training academy to public museum and, as a result of Napoleon's Italian campaigns, great works such as the *Medici Venus* and Raphael's *Marriage of the Virgin* were among the loot that was brought back to Paris. In 1802 Napoleon I decided to reform the museum's administration by putting Baron Denon in charge and assigned the architects Percier and Fontaine to renovate and improve the building. The Cour Carrée was finished off, the Carrousel Arch was built, and the North Gallery along Rue de Rivoli extended.

The fate of the museum followed the political vagaries of France, and after Napoleon I's downfall many works were returned to their countries of origin. On the other hand, the collections were bolstered by purchases and donations, and new rooms were opened. The whole project came together between 1852 and 1871, during the Second Empire, when Napoleon III created the New Louvre, adding courtyards north and south of Cour Napoleon. On 14 August 1857 the new palace-museum on the Seine side, designed specifically to house the collections, was inaugurated, its main entrance in Denon wing, and ministries and public services offices were installed in the northern section. During the Commune riots in 1871 the Rivoli wing was set ablaze but subsequently restored, whereas the Tuileries Palace was lost forever.

The culmination was the Grand Louvre Project initiated by President Mitterand, which began in 1983. Part of the project was the new main entrance, in the shape of the controversial glass Pyramid designed by Ieoh Ming Pei, which has become the most emblematic of 20c Parisian buildings.

MEDIEVAL LOUVRE

The excavation of the Cour Carrée in 1983-4 removed 16,000 cubic metres of earth to expose the foundations of Philippe II Auguste's medieval fortress and the palace of Charles V, now called the Medieval Louvre. This section adds a fascinating dimension to our understanding of the building and its history. Moving through this twilight zone, you pass the remains of walls, the outer moat, various towers, including the Tour du Milieu (12c), and the remains of the eastern entrance to the Château. Inside the walls is the base of a circular *donjon* or keep (formerly 30m high), constructed at the turn of the 13c but later razed. Archaeological finds extracted from this site and from the Cour Napoleon reveal life in the old castle.

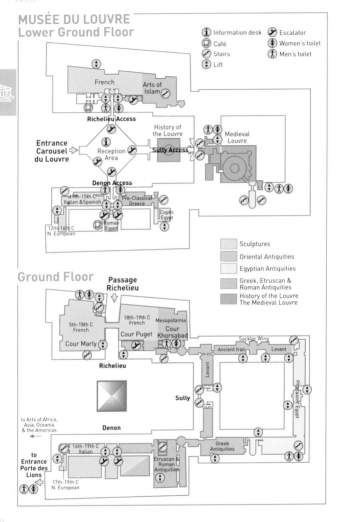

MUSÉE DU LOUVRE
Lower Ground Floor

- (i) Information desk
- (☕) Café
- (🚶) Stairs
- (🛗) Lift
- (↗) Escalator
- (🚺) Women's toilet
- (🚹) Men's toilet

French

Arts of Islam

Richelieu Access

Entrance Carousel du Louvre

Reception Area

History of the Louvre

Sully Access

Medieval Louvre

Denon Access

11th–15th C Italian & Spanish

Pre-Classical Greece

Coptic Egypt

12th–16th C N. European

Roman Egypt

Sculptures

Oriental Antiquities

Egyptian Antiquities

Greek, Etruscan & Roman Antiquities

History of the Louvre / The Medieval Louvre

Ground Floor

Passage Richelieu

5th–18th C French

Cour Marly

18th–19th C French

Cour Puget

Mesopotamia

Cour Khorsabad

Richelieu

Sackler Wing

Ancient Iran

Levant

Levant

Sully

Pharaonic Egypt

Denon

Greek Antiquities

to Arts of Africa, Asia, Oceania & the Americas

to Entrance Porte des Lions

16th–19th C Italian

Etruscan & Roman Antiquities

17th–19th C N. European

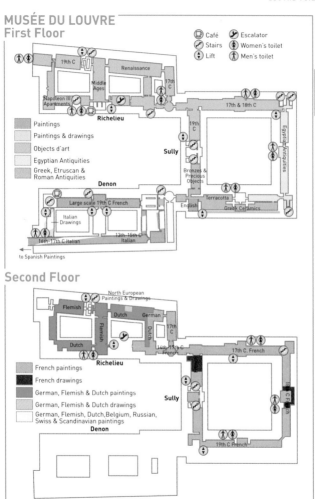

MUSÉE DU LOUVRE
First Floor

Café · Escalator
Stairs · Women's toilet
Lift · Men's toilet

19th C · Renaissance · 17th C

Middle Ages

Napoleon III Apartments

Richelieu

17th & 18th C

Paintings
Paintings & drawings
Objects d'art
Egyptian Antiquities
Greek, Etruscan & Roman Antiquities

19th C

Sully

Egyptian Antiquities

Bronzes & Precious Objects

Denon

Large scale 19th C French

Italian Drawings

16th-17th C Italian · 13th-15th C Italian

English · Terracotta · Greek Ceramics

to Spanish Paintings

Second Floor

North European Paintings & Drawings

Flemish · Dutch · German · 17th C

Flemish

Dutch

Richelieu

14th-15th C French

17th C. French

French paintings
French drawings
German, Flemish & Dutch paintings
German, Flemish & Dutch drawings
German, Flemish, Dutch, Belgium, Russian, Swiss & Scandinavian paintings

Sully

17th C. French

Denon

19th C French

FRENCH PAINTING
HIGHLIGHTS

Portrait of Jean Le Bon   Room 1

Works by Georges de la Tour   Rooms 28-29

Rococo works by Watteau and Boucher
Still lifes by Chardin   Rooms 36-40

Works by Ingres   Room 60

Large works by David, Géricault and Delacroix   Rooms 75, 77

14C-17C: RICHELIEU SECOND FLOOR

ROOMS 1-17 The first three rooms are devoted to International Gothic, common to both French and Northern European Schools, which was developed by Franco-Flemish artists working in Paris, Dijon and Bourges between about 1370 and 1450. It is characterized by elegance, decorative refinement and a celebration of courtly life, as well as a charming attention to naturalistic details. These aspects are combined in the *Carrying of the Cross* by Jacquemart de Hesdin and in the *Retable* from the Chapelle Cardon (c 1400).

Avignon was the seat of the papal court in the 14c and produced brilliant works such as the *Thouzon Retable* (c 1410). A bold and simplified form of portraiture was practised by **Jean Fouquet** (c 1420-80) - see his depiction of *Charles VII* - and was dominated in the 16c by **Jean Clouet** (c 1485-c 1541), who painted a portrait of *François I*.

The Schools of Fontainebleau (16c) show the influence of the Italian Renaissance on French paintings.

ROOMS 12, 19, 31 Characteristic of the 17c are the confident works of court painters during the reigns of Louis XIII and Louis XIV. Simon Vouet (1590-1649), who produced many altarpieces, delighted in golden yellows. **Philippe de Champaigne** (1602-74), deeply influenced by the austere Jansenist sect, painted *The Echevins of the City of Paris* (1648) and *Two Nuns of Port Royal* (1662) whereas in contrast **Le Brun**'s (1619-90) *Equestrian Portrait of Chancellor Seguier* (c 1661) is a sumptuous affair.

ROOMS 13, 14, 16-19 A series of rooms is filled with the often rigorous and intellectual work of **Nicolas Poussin** (1594-1665). The Louvre owns 38 Poussins, a quarter of the existing total, which include *The Arcadian Shepherds* (c 1650) and *Apollo and Daphne* (1664). It has fewer of the more atmospheric landscapes by his counterpart **Le Lorrain (Claude)** (c 1600-82), such as the *Arrival of Cleopatra at Tarsa* (1642-3).

17C-19C: SULLY SECOND FLOOR
ROOMS 20-23 Rotating exhibitions of French Graphic Arts.

ROOMS A, B, C Three very fine collections - Beistegui, Lyon and Cröy - with works dating from the 17c-19c, encompass landscapes by Northern and Venetian artists, portraits by **Fragonard**, **Van Dyck**, and **Rubens**, and a selection of **Impressionist** paintings.

ROOMS 24-25, 28-29, 32-35 Numerous genre scenes include works by **Georges de la Tour** (1593-1652) who was inspired by northern followers of Caravaggio. He is best known for compositions where the drama is heightened by the effect of candlelight, as well as deliciously anecdotal works such as *The Card-sharper*.

ROOMS 36-40, 43-49 Among favourites by **Antoine Watteau** (1694-1721) from Flanders, who learned theatrical scene painting in Paris, are the monumental but enigmatic *Gilles*, a Pierrot from Italian or French comedy, and *Pilgrimage to Cythera*, a vision of a lazy, hedonistic day in late summer, described as a *fête galante*. Examples of the tranquil still lifes for which **Jean-Baptiste-Siméon Chardin** (1699-1779) was famous are *Le Buffet*, a pyramid of reds and greys, and *The Ray*. He also painted studies of children. Quite different are the frothy nudes for which **François Boucher** (1703-70) is renowned, such as *Diana getting out of her*

Bath. 18c portraits, landscapes and vibrant, light-hearted themes by **Jean-Honoré Fragonard** (1732-1806) include *Le Verrou* and a portrait of *Marie-Madeleine Guimard*.

ROOMS 51-63 A remarkably successful and courageous portraitist, **Elisabeth Vigée-Lebrun** (1755-1842) became a favourite of Marie Antoinette, and was to travel throughout Europe after the Revolution, living off her earnings (and good connections). The uncompromising Neoclassical style of **Jacques Louis David** (1748-1825), whose political loyalties changed with the tide, influenced French painting via his pupils Baron A.-J. Gros, Baron François Gérard and Ingres.

   Jean Auguste Dominique Ingres (1780-1867), a consummate draughtsman, was a hugely successful portraitist whose style barely altered during his long career. He was especially famous for the voluptuous Oriental scenes inspired by North Africa, such as *The Turkish Bath* and the *Bather of Valpinçon*, as well as more sober religious paintings.

   Great Romantic painters include the technically innovative **Théodore Géricault** (1791-1824) who painted directly on the canvas without the help of preparatory studies and whose subjects ranged from politically controversial incidents to horses and wild animals. **Eugène Delacroix** (1789-1863), the major painter of the Romantic movement, stylistically opposite to his arch rival, the classicist Ingres, was a remarkable colourist who many of the later-19c artists, such as the Impressionists and Van Gogh, held in great esteem.

ROOMS 64-72 Two major collections, Moreau-Nélaton and Thomy-Thiery, contain examples of the silvery landscapes which are the hallmark of **J.-B. Corot** (1796-1875), a typical scene of peasant life by the painter **J.-F. Millet** (1814-75), and works by the Barbizon artists, among the first to work in the open-air.

LARGE 19C PAINTINGS: DENON FIRST FLOOR
ROOMS 75, 77 Epic and theatrical works are gathered in these rooms. **David**'s work, inspired by antiquity, *The Oath of the Horatii*

Jean Auguste Dominique Ingres *Bather* (1828)

(1784), was widely seen as extolling Republican virtues although commissioned for the Crown. On display is his brilliant historical record of *The Coronation of Napoleon I in Notre-Dame, 2 December 1804* (1805-7), and striking portraits such as *M. Sériziat, his Wife*

and *Son*, and *Madame Recamier* (1800), who launched the vogue for the Empire style in the early 19c. **Ingres**' haughtily chaste reclining nude, *Grande Odalisque* (1814) is a pool of tranquillity among other major Romantic paintings such as *Bonaparte visiting the Plague-striken at Jaffa* (1804) by **Baron Gros**; and **Delacroix**'s turbulent and colourful *Death of Sardanapolos* (1828) and *Liberty leading the People* (1830). The dramatic shipwreck captured by **Géricault**, *The Raft of the Medusa* (1819), was based on a contemporary event when 150 survivors struggled to survive on an improvised raft.

DUTCH, FLEMISH AND GERMAN PAINTING
HIGHLIGHTS

Religious paintings by Rogier van der Weyden and Jan van Eyck	Rooms 4, 5
Works by Albrecht Dürer and Hans Holbein the Younger	Room 8
Médicis Cycle by Rubens	Room 18
Works by Rembrandt van Rijn	Room 31
Works by Vermeer	Room 38

15C-17C: RICHELIEU SECOND FLOOR

ROOMS 4-10 15c Dutch, Flemish and German painters broke away from the constraints and superficiality of International Gothic to produce works with deeper emotional content. Intense feeling is expressed in vibrant colour by **Rogier van der Weyden** (c 1399-64) in the *Braque Family Triptych* (c 1450) and *Annunciation*. **Jan van Eyck** (active 1422-41), *Virgin with Chancellor Nicolas Rolin* presents the rich and powerful Chancellor of Burgundy as donor of this exceptional composition. *The Ship of Fools* by Hieronymus Bosch (active 1474-1516) is a typically strange representation by this artist.

German paintings, from Cologne and other artistic centres, include *Self-Portrait* (1523), by one of the greatest draughtsman of all time, **Albrecht Dürer** (1471-1528), and five magnificent portraits by **Hans Holbein the Younger** (1497-1543), including *Anne of Cleves* and *Erasmus*. Representative of 16c Netherlandish painters is **Quentin Metsys** (1465-1530), *Moneylender and his Wife* - note the reflection in the round mirror.

ROOMS 13, 15, 17-26 16c-17c Flemish painting was dominated by **Peter-Paul Rubens** (1577-1640) and **Anthony van Dyck** (1599-1641). In a specially designed gallery is Rubens' resplendent series of 24 huge allegorical works depicting the *Life of Marie de Médicis* (1622-5), designed for the Luxembourg Palace.

In the other rooms are huge religious paintings by Jacob Jordaens (1593-1678), Van Dyck and (across Escalier Lefuel) further works by Rubens, including a tenderly executed portrait of his wife *Hélène Fourment with Two of her Children*. By Van Dyck are *Venus and Vulcan* (1626-32), painted just before his departure for England, and the brilliant portrait of *Charles I of England* (c 1637).

ROOMS 27-31 16c-17c Dutch paintings here emphasize the variety and wealth of the Dutch School. Magnificent portraits by **Frans Hals** (1581/85-1666), landscapes by Solomon van Ruysdael (1600/03-70), and large history paintings by Caravaggist artists are exhibited alongside more sober works by Ter Brugghen (1588-1629). The richly textured, mystical works of **Rembrandt van Rijn** (1606-69), include two *Self-Portraits* of 1633, and the *Artist in his Old Age at his Easel* (1660). From the 'Baroque' years, 1630-40, a period where Rembrandt produced works of heightened drama and intensity are the *Archangel Raphael taking leave of the Family of Tobias*, and the *Holy Famil*y. More mature are *Christ at Emmaus* (1648), *St Matthew and the Angel* (1661), while perhaps the best known of the Louvre Rembrandt's is the monumental, copper-toned *Bathsheba Bathing* (1654).

ROOMS 32-39 The mid to end of the 17c Dutch paintings include followers of Rembrandt and landscapes and still lifes. Two virtuoso paintings by **Jan Vermeer** (1632-75) stand out, *The Lacemaker* (c 1679), and *The Astronomer*, intense, intimate compositions which use a subtle play of light and delicate colours.

ROOM A-F 18c-19c Northern European paintings including Russian, Swiss and Scandinavian.

ITALIAN PAINTING
HIGHLIGHTS

Florentine painters, Giotto to Botticelli — Room 3

Italian High Renaissance, Leonardo da Vinci — Room 5

Roman School, represented by Raphael — Room 8

Baroque period, Caravaggio — Room 12

Leonardo's *Mona Lisa* (temporary setting) — Room 13

Venetian paintings (temporary setting) — Room 74, 76

14C-18C: DENON FIRST FLOOR

ROOM 1-2 Very elegant 15c and early 16c frescoes by Botticelli, and Fra Angelico.

ROOM 3 Florentine masters of the 13c-15c made early experiments in depicting depth and naturalism. These aspects were explored by **Cimabue** (c 1240-1302), and expanded on by **Giotto** (c 1266-1337) as in *St Francis Receiving the Stigmata*. The great 15c Florentine **Fra Angelico** (c 1400-55) portrays a triumphant *Coronation of the Virgin*. Paolo Uccello (c 1396-1475), *Battle of San Romano* (1432), is a colourful if charmingly wooden battle scene. **Sandro Botticelli** (1445-1510), the most important Florentine artist of the second half of the 15c, painted the refined and delicate *Madonna and Child surrounded by Angels*.

ROOM 4 Siena and Northern Italy, 13c-15c, are represented by Pisanello (c 1395-1454) and **Piero della Francesca** (c 1416-92), whose intellectually rigorous style and predilection for sharp profiles is revealed in *Portrait of Sigismondo Malatesta*. Small works include one by **Simone Martini** (c 1284-1344) from Siena, who worked for a time in Avignon, *Christ bearing the Cross* (c 1342).

ROOMS 5, 8, 12 The Grande Galerie in Denon, a relic of Napoleon III's museum, contains 15c-16c Renaissance works of outstanding beauty.

Tuscany and northern Italy are represented by the precise draughtsmanship of **Andrea Mantegna** (c 1430-1506) in *Crucifixion* and *St Sebastian*; also by **Ghirlandaio** (1449-94), *The Bottlenosed old Man and his Grandson*.

From the Venetian School, **Giovanni Bellini** (c 1430-1516) raised Venetian art to a level equal to that of Florence. You can see here his *Crucifixion* and *Virgin and Child with Saints*. From Perugia in Umbria, **Perugino** (c 1445-1523), Raphael's master, depicted *The Madonna and Child with St Catherine and St John the Baptist*.

The end of the Quattrocento (15c) and first quarter of the Cinquecento (16c), the period of the Italian High Renaissance, was the moment when perfect harmony and proportion came together to produce some of the greatest Italian art.

The Louvre has a fine collection of works by **Leonardo da Vinci** (1452-1519) which are endowed with an aura of mystery and sensuality. Such atmosphere envelopes the *Virgin of the Rocks* (1482), similar to but probably earlier than the London version, and the tender and close-knit group of three generations, *Madonna and Child with St Anne*. Here are also his *Annunciation*, *St John the Baptist* and *La Belle Ferronnière* (named after the metal chain around her neck).

Younger than Leonardo, the leader of the Roman School was Raffaello Sanzio, called **Raphael** (1483-1520). *La Belle Jardinière* (1507) is heavy with religious symbolism, and one of several such Holy Family groups, in which he echoes the pyramidal composition favoured by Leonardo. The proud *Portrait of Baldassare Castiglione*, poet and diplomat, was purchased by Louis XIV in 1661 from the heirs of Cardinal Mazarin. Giulio Romano (c 1499-1546), who trained with Raphael, was, like his master, also an architect. He produced the sumptuous portrait of the *Vice-Queen of Naples*. **Correggio** (c 1489-1534), the master of *sfumato* (the very subtle graduation of tones) and had a talent for religious subjects which are both tender and voluptuous. The archetypal exponent of the exaggerated forms of Mannerism was

Jacopo **Pontormo** (1494-1557), *Virgin and Child with Saint Anne and Four Saints*. Arcimboldo (1527-93) painted curious 'portraits' of fruit and vegetables.

ROOM 6, off the Grande Galerie, normally contains Venetian paintings, including glorious works of dynamic colour, the peak of Venetian art by **Titian** (c 1485-1576) in *Lady at her Toilet* and *Venus of the Pardo* as well as the gentle *Concert Champêtre*. **Tintoretto** (1518-94) combined the colour of Titian and the drawing of Michelangelo in works such as *Paradise*. Paolo Veronese's (1528-88) huge *Marriage at Cana* is temporarily in Room 76.

ROOMS 9-10 16c and 17c Italian cartoons and drawings exhibited in rotation.

ROOM 12 The greatest Italian painter of the late 16c, **Caravaggio** (1571-1610) was notorious in his private life and passionate in his work. *The Fortune-Teller* seems to be giving a clear message of things to come, and *Death of the Virgin* (1605-6) was considered scandalous at the time because of the earthy realism of the figures. Also exhibited here are works by the most talented of the Bolognese **Carracci family**, Annibale (1560-1609); and large paintings by Guido Reni (1575-1642), who was influenced by the Carracci.

ROOM 13 (Temporary setting) The most famous work in the Louvre is **Leonardo da Vinci**'s celebrated portrait of the mysterious, enigmatic and slightly smug *Mona Lisa* (1503-6) in hazy mountain scenery. Also known as *La Gioconda* (in French, *La Joconde*), it is traditionally assumed to represent Mona Lisa Gherardini, third wife of Francesco di Zanobi del Giocondo. The painter brought it to France when he was invited here by François I in 1516. The rest of the large gallery contains works by Salvator Rosa (1615-73), from Naples, prototype Romantic artist, but hard pushed to compete with the Mona Lisa.

ROOMS 23-25 Venetian scenes by **Canaletto** (1697-1768), including *The Molo* (c 1730), of which there are about 10 versions, and Francesco Guardi (1712-93) who used a freer and more expressive mood for his Venice-scapes. **Tiepolo** (1696-1770), the last in a line of fresco artists, produced exuberant yet decorative work, as in *The Last Supper*.

ENGLISH PAINTING
DENON FIRST FLOOR

ROOM 74 (Temporary setting) This small but high-quality collection contains works by **John Constable** (1776-1837), *Weymouth Bay*; **J.M.W. Turner** (1775-1851), *Landscape with a River and a Bay* (c 1845); and by important 18c portraitists such as Joshua Reynolds (1723-92), Thomas Gainsborough (1727-88), and George Romney (1734-1802). The landscape painter, Richard Parkes Bonington (1801/2-28), who spent much of his short life in France, is also represented.

SPANISH PAINTING
HIGHLIGHTS
Works by Goya

Room 32

DENON FIRST FLOOR (EXTREME WEST)

ROOM 26 This is not a vast collection, but it is notable for a series of masterpieces. The Murillo Room is dedicated to the Golden Age of Spanish painting (17c-18c). Brought together here are seven large works of **Bartolomé Estabán Murillo** (1618-82), who was known for his sweet Madonnas. *The Angels' Kitchen* is one of a series painted for the Franciscan convent at Seville, *Birth of the Virgin* has typically soft colouring, and *Young Beggar* (1650) is an example of Murillo's later theme of picturesque urchins. Overall **Francisco de Zurbarán** (1598-1664) was a more sombre painter, *St Bonaventura at the Council of Lyon*, *St Bonaventure's Corpse Exposed*; and a delightful *St Apollinaire*. **El Greco** (1541-1614), is represented by a characteristic work of heavy pathos, *Crucifixion with two Donors* (signed in Greek characters) c 1579.

21

ROOM 27-29 15c-16c masterpieces from Valencia, Catalonia and Castille include works by the Master of Burgo de Osma (early 15c), retable with the *Virgin and Child*; Jaime Huguet, *Flagellation and Lamentation*; and Francisco Collantes (1599-1656), *The Burning Bush*.

ROOM 30 17c works by the great **Diego Velázquez** (1599-1660), include *Queen Mariana of Austria*; portrait of the *Infanta Margarita*, aged three years.

ROOM 32 Francisco Goya (1746-1828), whose ability to absorb a variety of influences made him the most original artist of his period. Gathered here are the striking portrait of *Ferdinand Guillemardet* (c 1798), *Woman with a Fan* (c 1810), and portraits of *Mariana Waldstein*, *Marquesa de Santa Cruz* and *Evaristo Pérez de Castro*.

GREEK AND RUSSIAN ICONS

ROOM 31 Mainly 16c-17c. Includes examples of the Cretan School, end 15c-early 16c, and Russian, 16c, such as *The Virgin of Georgia* from Novgorod.

PRINTS AND DRAWINGS

These works are fragile and susceptible to light and are therefore exhibited in rotation every 3-6 months. They are divided between the appropriate schools of painting: **French School**, Sully second floor (Rooms 20-23, 41, 42, 44, 45); **Northern Schools**, Richelieu second floor (Room 12); **Italian Schools**, Denon first floor, Mollien Wing (Rooms 9-10).

FRENCH SCULPTURE
HIGHLIGHTS

Tomb of Philippe Pot   Room 10

Works by Michel Colombe   Room 11

Germain Pilon, *Virgin of Sorrows*   Room 14

Works by Antoine Coysevox and Guillaume Coustou   Cour Marly

Works by Pierre Puget   Cour Puget
Works by David d'Angers

Works by François Rude   Rooms 32-33

RICHELIEU LOWER GROUND & GROUND FLOORS

This section is organized around Cour Marly and Cour Puget, the courtyards which were glazed and terraced in 1993 creating well-lit spaces for the display of large sculptures originally designed for royal gardens or public places.

6C-14C ROMANESQUE AND GOTHIC SCULPTURES *Rooms 1-9*

Outstanding is the *Courajod Christ* (12c) in wood, from Burgundy, and an interesting *Head of St Peter* (12c), with eyes of inlaid lead, from the tomb of St Lazarus, Autun. The intermediary period, mid-12c to early-13c, between Romanesque and Gothic, is characterized by the *Annunciation* and *Visitation* on a capital from the Paris area. An elegant piece of 13c Gothic sculpture, *St Matthew Dictated to by the Angel*, is thought to be a fragment from the choir screen of Chartres Cathedral. The display of 14c religious sculpture includes the remarkable relief of *Canon Pierre de Fayel* (d. 1344) from Notre-Dame. Funerary monuments typical of 14c French sculpture include the Blanchelande *Virgin and Child* from Basse-Normandie, the first medieval work to be acquired by the Louvre in 1850.

Among mid-14c to early 15c sculptures from the from Ile de France and Berry are small statues for the tomb of the entrails of King Charles IV (le Bel, d. 1324) and his queen, Jeanne d'Evreux (d. 1371), by Jean de Liège.

15C SCULPTURE FROM BURGUNDY AND THE LOIRE *Rooms 10-11*

These two important artistic centres developed along different lines. From the first is the celebrated *Tomb of Philippe Pot* (d. 1493), Grand Seneschal of Burgundy, supported by eight *pleurants* (weepers). **Michel Colombe** (c 1430-c 1512), from the Loire, made the superb marble high-relief of *St George and the Dragon* (1504-9), commissioned by Georges d'Amboise for the Château of Gallon. Colombe's influence in the region is obvious in the *Tomb of René d'Orléans-Longueville* (d. 1515).

EARLY-16C FUNERARY MONUMENTS *Room 12* From the Ile de France and Champagne, a hugely ornate Flamboyant retable of the *Resurrection*, and the death statue from the Auvergne of *Jeanne de Bourbon, Comtesse d'Auvergne*, 1521, being gruesomely devoured by worms.

ROYAL RESIDENCES & FUNERARY MONUMENTS *Room 14-19* Inspired by antiquity and the Italian Renaissance, the most outstanding sculptors of the 16c were **Pierre Bontemps** (c 1505-c 1568), **Jean Goujon** (c 1510-64/9), the base of the *Fountain of Innocents*, 1547-9, and **Germain Pilon** (c 1531-90), whose terracotta model for the *Virgin of Sorrows* is a remarkable survival from a commission by Queen Catherine de Médicis for the Valois chapel at St-Denis (but never built). Barthélemy Prieur succeeded Pilon, continuing in a more sober style, and his *Fontaine de Diane* (upper part) from the Château of Anet is the oldest surviving garden sculpture in France.

The monument of the *Pont-au-Change* (17c), **Simon Guillain**'s masterpiece, dominated the busy crossroads opposite the Cité at the time of Louis XIII (1610-54).

PARC DE MARLY *Cour Marly* The courtyard is named after the sculptures from the Parc de Marly, Louis XIV's private retreat. The architect **Jules Hardouin-Mansart** (1646-1708) embellished the gardens with complicated water features and exuberant examples of Rococo sculptures by leading artists. **Antoine Coysevox** (1640-1720) was responsible for part of the cascade featuring *Seine, Marne, Neptune and Amphitrite*, and the equestrian groups, *Mercury and Fame* (1699-1702) (upper level), which were transferred to the Tuileries in 1719. These were superseded by the magnificent *Marly Horses* (1743-5) by **Guillaume 1er Coustou** (1677-1746), which were subsequently moved to the end of the Champs-Elysées (now replaced by reproductions).

17C-18C SCULPTURE *Room 20* In the gallery (Crypte Giradon) between the courtyards are works by Giradon, Puget, and Coysevox. These include a small model for the equestrian statue of Louis XIV by François Girardon (1628-1715) and a marble relief by Pierre Puget (1620-94), *The Meeting of Alexander and Diogenes* (1671-89), made for Louis XIV.

17C-19C SCULPTURE *Cour Puget* Scattered through this charming space is a disparate collection which includes monuments for public places and parks, although **Pierre Puget**'s *Milon of Crotona* (1671-82) and *Perseus and Andromeda* (1687-94) were destined for Versailles. Beneath the trees are 17c sculptures by Sébastien Slodtz (1655-1726) and Nicolas Coustou (1658-1733). Coysevox's lighthearted piece, *Marie-Adelaide de Savoie, Duchesse de Bourgogne*, portrays the mother of Louis XV as Diana (1710), while **Jean-Baptiste Pigalle**'s (1714-85) *Madame de Pompadour en Amitié*, marble, 1753, is Louis XV's favourite with flowers of all seasons.

MID 18C-19C *Rooms 21-30* On the terrace are works for the open-air, and in the first-floor galleries on the north side of the courtyard are small format works. J.-B. Pigalle produced the exceptionally elaborate model for the mausoleum of Marshall Saxe, Strasbourg, in its architectural setting, *Voltaire Nu* in marble, 1776, and *Self Portrait* in terracotta. High in drama but small in scale are qualifying works for acceptance at the Académie royale de Peinture et de Sculpture from 1704 to 1791. The portraitists, J.-J. Caffieri (1725-92) and his rival Augustin Pajou (1730-1809) were eclipsed by **J.-A. Houdon** (1741-1828) whose busts include *Voltaire*, the singer *Sophie Arnould*, and *George Washington*. The Gallery of Grands Hommes has statues of illustrious men commissioned in 1776 during the reign of Louis XVI.

REVOLUTION, EMPIRE AND RESTORATION *Room 31* Wonderfully ostentatious are the silver and bronze *Peace*, conceived by Vivant

Denon, Director of the Louvre, and modelled by Chaudet (1763-1810); *Napoleon I in Coronation Robes*, marble, 1813, by Ramey (1754-1838); a mosaic by Belloni (1772-1863), with the hardly modest title *The Genius of the Emperor, Controlling Victory, brings back Peace and Abundance*, 1810, was designed for the Louvre.

ROMANTIC WORKS, 1820-50 *Rooms 32-33 and Cour Puget Upper Level* Well executed but sentimental, a few verging on the downright silly, are pieces by James Pradier (1790-1852) and others. A certain amount of individuality shines through in **David d'Angers'** (1788-1856) *Child with the Bunch of Grapes* (1845) and large portrait heads in marble, at which he excelled. Works by the famous animal sculptor **A.-L. Barye** (1795-1875) include his best-known *Jaguar devouring a Hare*, and *Roger and Angelique riding the Hippogriffe*. One of the greatest of the period was **François Rude** (1784-1855), *Mercury and Young Neapolitan playing with a Turtle*. *Joan of Arc Hearing Voices* was commissioned in 1845 for a series of illustrations of women for the Luxembourg Gardens.

ITALIAN SCULPTURE
HIGHLIGHTS

Works by Donatello and studio   Room 1

Michelangelo's *Slaves*   Room 4

DENON LOWER GROUND FLOOR & GROUND FLOOR

6C-15C *Room 1* Several images of the Madonna and Child, in a variety of materials such as the life-size version in painted wood by Jacopo della Quercia (c 1374-1438). Dominating Italian sculpture in the 15c are the elegant and sensual works of the great **Donatello** (c 1386-1466). His *Madonna and Child*, in coloured and gilded terracotta, is a figure of great delicacy and pathos. A prime example of marble low relief is the *Virgin surrounded by Four Angels* by Agostino di Duccio (1418-81), sculpted for Piero de Medici. Masterly are the three reliefs of the *Madonna and Child*, by Mino da Fiesole (1418-81), which give the effect of transparent fabrics.

DELLA ROBBIA WORKSHOP *Room 2* A collection of enamelled earthenware, in characteristic blue and white or yellow and green, from the Florentine workshop of the Della Robbia family (Luca, 1399/1400-1482; Andrea, 1435-1525; Giovanni, 1469-1529) and Benedetto Buglioni (1459-1521).

On the staircase landing is the large *Nymph of Fontainebleau*, a bronze bas-relief by **Benvenuto Cellini** (1500-72), made for the Porte d'Orée at Fontainebleau but placed, until the Revolution, above the gateway of the Château d'Anet.

MICHELANGELO GALLERY *Room 4* This a suitably grand setting for the most celebrated works in the department, **Michelangelo Buonarotti**'s (1475-1564) two Slaves of 1513-15: *The Captive*, struggling for his freedom, and the sensuous *Dying Slave*. Both were intended for the tomb of Pope Julius II in Rome, but given to Henri II in 1550 by Robert Strozzi and placed for some time at the Château d'Ecouen before passing into Cardinal Richelieu's collection.

Of the High Baroque period, works by **Bernini** (1598-1680) include *Angel carrying the Crown of Thorns* (terracotta, Rome c 1667); and the *Bust of Cardinal Richelieu*, modelled on the triple portrait of Richelieu (in the National Gallery, London) by Philippe de Champaigne.

At the end of the gallery are works by **Antonio Canova** (1757-1822), *Psyche revived by the Kiss of Cupid*, and *Cupid and Psyche*.

SPANISH SCULPTURE
DENON LOWER GROUND FLOOR

12C-18C *Room 3* A small collection of works is squeezed between the Italian and the Northern section, with capitals from the Visigothic and Mozarab periods; works in alabaster from royal tombs in Poblet; an extraordinary work illustrating a Franciscan legend, the *Dead St Francis* (mid-17c?), in wood with eyes of glass, teeth of bone, and cord of hemp.

NORTHERN SCULPTURE
DENON LOWER GROUND FLOOR

12C-16C *Rooms A, B, C* English 15C alabasters from Nottingham; International Gothic Virgins (12c-15c); a 12c Bavarian *Crucifixion* carved in lime wood, the emaciated and touching figure of Christ wearing a long pleated perizonium; a celebrated *Virgin and Child* from Isenheim, near Colmar, originally the central part of a retable carved in lime wood; a handful of German and Dutch works from the later Gothic period, 15c-16c.

ORIENTAL ANTIQUITIES
HIGHLIGHTS

Stela of the Vultures	Room 1a
Statues of Prince Gudea	Room 2
Codex of the Hammurabi (temporarily in Room 4)	Room 3
Khorsabad Courtyard, *Winged Bulls*	Room 4
Lady of Batriana	Room 9
Ivory pyxis	Room B
Moabite stone or *Stela of Mesha*	Room D

RICHELIEU GROUND FLOOR

ANCIENT MESOPOTAMIA AND SUMERIAN CULTURE *Rooms 1a, 1b, 1c* (Origins to 3rd millennium BC.) Small objects remarkable for both their age and beauty. Most finds are from Tello, formerly Girsu (Iraq), and Mari, dating from before 3000 BC. The *Cylinder of Uruk* (c 3100 BC) is one of the earliest examples of a seal-cylinder used to 'sign' documents. Hieroglyphics demonstrate the spread of writing (c 2900-2340 BC). One of the oldest known historical documents, the magnificent limestone *Stela of the Vultures*, c 2450 BC (restored), from Tello, records the victory of Eannatum, King of Lagash. Mesopotamian culture spread in particular to Mari, on the modern Iraq-Syria border, where excavations at the temple of the goddess Ishtar (c 2500 BC) produced important pieces.

ANCIENT MESOPOTAMIA (2350-2000 BC) *Room 2* The Empire of
Akkad is represented by objects from Susa (the capital, Akkad
never having been found), moved there in the 12c BC, its glory
idealized in royal diorite monuments, the most beautiful being the
Stela of the Victorious Naram-Sin, king of Akkad. In cabinets are
minutely carved seal-cylinders and Akkadian judicial documents,
with their 'print-outs' in clay. The brilliant second Dynasty of
Lagash (2150-2100 BC) is represented by nine diorite *statues of
prince Gudea*, showing him holding a vase from which gushes life-
giving water, and by large clay cylinders recording, in cuneiform,
Gudea's achievements.

MESOPOTAMIA (2000-1000 BC) *Room 3* (The *Codex of Hammurabi* is
temporarily in Room 4.) Mural paintings from the Amorite Palace
of King Zimri-Lim, Mari, and an imagined reconstruction of the
palace; bronze lion from Mari. The first Babylonian Empire
developed under King Hammurabi (c 1792-50 BC), when the
freestanding *Codex of Hammurabi* was carved in black basalt and
covered with closely written text comprising 282 laws which
embrace practically every aspect of Babylonian life. After the
king's death Babylon declined, but its brilliance revived during the
neo-Babylonian Empire. Its greatest king was Nebuchadnezzar II
(605-562 BC), who captured Jerusalem, deported the Jews, and
erected magnificent buildings. Objects of the period include the
coloured glazed-brick frieze, *Lion Passant*, which decorated a
processional route between temples; the *Astrological Calendar* of
Uruk; a series of alabaster *Statuettes of Female Nudes* showing the
influence of Hellenic culture after Babylon was conquered in 331
BC by Alexander the Great.

MESOPOTAMIA AND ASSYRIA *Room 4* Cour Khorsabad contains
celebrated reliefs from the great Assyrian palace of Khorsabad.
The Assyrian Empire reached its peak between the 9c and 7c BC,
and its rulers built great palaces to celebrate their achievements.
The impressive presentation against the walls of the courtyard is
designed to evoke the original massive scale of the Palace of Dur-
Sharrukin, Sargon II's fortress (Khorsabad). The five huge *Winged
Bulls* with human heads, or *lamassu*, stood at the entrances to

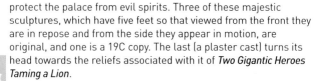

protect the palace from evil spirits. Three of these majestic sculptures, which have five feet so that viewed from the front they are in repose and from the side they appear in motion, are original, and one is a 19C copy. The last (a plaster cast) turns its head towards the reliefs associated with it of *Two Gigantic Heroes Taming a Lion*.

HITTITE EMPIRE *Room 5* This room contains objects from the Anatolian, Cappadocian (parts of present-day Turkey) and Hittite civilizations up to 1000 BC. Anatolia was on a major route between Asia and the West and its mineral wealth was such that traders overcame the difficulties of transport, and at the same time brought their own cultural influences to the region. Around 1650 BC a Hittite prince brought together under his authority most of the small kingdoms of Central Anatolia or Cappadocia. This Empire became one of the great powers of the Near East in the 17c-13c BC, rivalling even Egypt.

MESOPOTAMIA AND ASSYRIA *Room 6* Artefacts from Assyrian provincial palaces include rare mural paintings from Til Barsip (present day Tell Ahmar, northern Syria) one featuring a *Blue Goat*; and an exceptional collection of carved ivories from Arslan Tash. There are also reliefs from the palace of Ashur at Nineveh (668-627 BC).

ANCIENT IRAN *Room 7-9* These rooms include works from ancient Iran (up to the 3rd millennium BC) of which Susa, the capital of the western part, was founded c 4200 BC. Three main artistic periods produced a range of artefacts: Susa I (4200-3800 BC), painted ceramics; Susa II or the period of Uruk (3800-3100 BC) saw the first attempts at metallurgy; Susa III (3100-2800 BC) the birth of proto-Elamite writing. Exhibits include the vase '*à la cachette*' (3rd millennium BC), discovered with treasure hidden inside it. From Luristan (Iran), to the north of Susa, are bronze arms and vessels (c 2600-1800 BC). Bactriana (Afghanistan) produced a wide range of objects, such as the remarkable statue of the *Lady of Bactriana* (c 1800 BC).

MIDDLE-ELAMITE IRAN (1500-1100 BC) *Room 10* Royal monuments of the reign of King Untash-Napirisha include a headless bronze statue of *Queen Napir Asu*, his wife, a considerable work weighing 1750kg. King Shutruk Nahhunte (12c BC) and his descendants were warrior kings and great builders, responsible for the acropolis of Susa from which are several architectural elements.

SULLY GROUND FLOOR - THE SACKLER WING

IRAN (14C BC-7C AD) *Rooms 11-16* These rooms contain items from **Iron Age Iran** (14c-6c BC), which was founded by nomadic horsemen who spoke an Indo-European language. Known as Iranians they assimilated something of Anatolian and Mesopotamian culture and later founded Persia. Items displayed show a stylized form of realism and include a vase in the form of a bull and a decorated horse's bit in bronze.

Of the great Persian **Achaemenid Empire** (6c-4c BC) are elements from the palace of Darius I at Susa, including a huge capital in the form of heads and shoulders of bulls, one of 36 used to support the ceiling of the audience chamber (*apadana*).

The **Parthian and Sassanian Empires** followed (3c BC-7c AD), represented by a mosaic of a harp player.

THE COUNTRIES OF THE LEVANT *Rooms A, B, C, D* These rooms contain a wealth of objects leading up to the Iron Age.

In **Cyprus**, important seams of copper and connections with the Hellenic world produced a characteristic style such as the Chalcolithic statuette, *Seated Female* (4th millennium); other delightful models include *Boat with Figures* (end 3rd millennium).

Coastal Syria is represented by furnishings from royal tombs and luxury items from Byblos, ceramics from Ras Shamra (ancient Ugarit) and objects from the tombs of Minet el Beida. These include an ivory pyxis carved with a goddess and two ibex (13c BC); also Phoenician sculptures and collections of objects such as an embossed gold peg, known as *The Hunt*, from Ras-Shamra.

Inland Syria absorbed influences from Mesopotamia to develop seal-cylinders, copper statuettes and the use of cuneiform writing. Also on display are the *Idol with Eyes*, in terracotta (c 35,000 BC) and a statue menhir in basalt from Tell Braq (2000-1600 BC).

Artefacts from **Palestine** (7000 BC-1150 BC) include a Neolithic plaster statue from Jericho, ivories from Beersheba (Negev), Bronze Age tomb furnishings from Jericho, Lakish, Ay and Farah, an ossuary in the form of a house, and a model of a sanctuary of the Israelite Dynasty (1200-1150 BC). The Moabite stone or *Stela of Mesha* (842 BC), was discovered in 1868 in a remote village east of the Dead Sea with a 34-line inscription recording victories over the Israelites in the reigns of Omri, Ahab and Ahaziah. This is one of the most important, if not the earliest, examples of alphabetic writing.

THE LEVANT *Rooms 17-21* (Following on from rooms A, B, C, D.) Brought together are present-day Syria, Lebanon, Israel, Jordan and Turkey at the cultural crossroads between the Mediterranean, Egypt and the distant Orient (1st millennium BC). A small area of the Levantine coast became known as **Phoenicia**. From the royal necropolis of the Phoenician kingdom at Sidon are sarcophagi and funerary monuments (8c-2c BC) and the *Stela of Amrit* (7c/8c BC).

With the Phoenician expansion to the west (8c-2c BC) around the Mediterranean, the culture of **Punic North Africa** developed (Punic was the language of Carthage related to Phoenicia), producing such pieces as the *Stela Tophet of Constantine* and glass objects.

Arabia Felix and the **Arabian desert** (7c-3c BC), which include present-day Yemen and the Syrian caravan cities of Palmyra and Dura Europos, yielded objects such as stele in alabaster, one with a human mask from Yemen; and from southern Syria the *Lintel of the Judgement of Paris* (2c BC), 3m long.

The complex mixture of cultures in **Cyprus** (9c-1c BC) is demonstrated by diverse works, dominated by the monumental *Vase of Amathonte*, carved from a single piece of limestone (3.2m in diameter) and used as a water reservoir for the sanctuary of the great goddess at the summit of the acropolis of Amathonte (4c BC).

ISLAMIC ART
RICHELIEU LOWER GROUND FLOOR

7C-10C *Rooms 1-2* The first appearance of Islamic art around the 7c-8c was a synthesis of Christian, Hellenistic and Sassanid (Persian) elements and is represented by objects in bronze, stucco and glass. The **Abbassid World** (8c-10c) created an imperial art derived from Greco-Roman and Sassanian traditions, mainly from Iraq, where lustreware was created in 9c-10c, but also from western Iran and Egypt.

10C-15C *Room 3* The **Fatimids** (909-1171) had a brilliant and refined culture which developed varied, often picturesque iconography in the decoration of small objects such as flasks and jewellery. From the **Islamic West** (10c-15c) is an outstanding ivory *Pyxis* (968) carved for al-Mughira, son of the Calif Abd al-Rahman III (912-961), during the Umayyad Caliphate in Cordoba, Andalusia.

IRAN 10C-13C *Rooms 4-6* The silk *Shroud of St Josse* (10c), from Khorasan, Eastern Iran, is decorated with elephants, camels and an inscription. It was brought to France after the first Crusade (1096-9).

Iran at the time of the Seljuks (11c-13c) was a high spot in the history of ceramics in the Muslim Orient demonstrated by an interesting series of 'provincial' ceramics decorated with champlevé and engraved slip. In a display dedicated to the sciences is a celestial sphere in brass inlaid with silver (1144), the oldest known of Arabic manufacture.

ROOM 7 Funerary stele and sculpted stones are arranged to represent a small rural cemetery (9c-18c).

ROOM 8 Objects from **Anatolia**, **Jezirah** and the **Syro-Egyptian world** (1250-1517), include the first examples of enamelled and gilded glass. The *Barberini Vase* was named after Pope Urban VIII Barberini to whom it was presented in the 17c.

One of the masterpieces of the Islamic collection (displayed separately), is the *Baptistère de Saint-Louis*, a hammered brass bowl, incised and inlaid with silver and gold (c 1300), first kept at the Sainte Chapelle of the Château of Vincennes.

ROOM 10 In the 13c-14c **China, Iran and the West** were in direct contact for the first time. A pale green dish with gilded fish is reminiscent of Chinese celadon glaze. The astrological motif of the lion and the sun became a national emblem in Iran in the 19c.

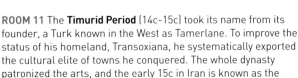

ROOM 11 The **Timurid Period** (14c-15c) took its name from its founder, a Turk known in the West as Tamerlane. To improve the status of his homeland, Transoxiana, he systematically exported the cultural elite of towns he conquered. The whole dynasty patronized the arts, and the early 15c in Iran is known as the Timurid Renaissance.

The **Safavid Period** (1501-1736) began with the conquest by Shah Isma'il of Azerbaïdjan and Iran. Local art was gradually penetrated by Western influences. Characteristic is the large *Mantes Carpet* (once at the Church of Mantes), decorated with animals and hunting scenes.

The **Qajar Period** (1779-1924) saw power pass to the Qajars who moved the political centre from Isfahan to Teheran. European influences penetrated and an important school of easel painting developed. Hence the portrait of the ruler, *Fath Ali Shah seated on the Peacock Throne*, received as a gift by Napoleon I.

From **Mughal India** (1526-1858) is a dagger with horse's head and a hookah (narghileh) of enamelled and gilded glass.

OTTOMAN WORLD 14C-19C *Room 12-13* Here is a large collection of Iznik ceramics showing all the variations of colour and motif used in these works. There are also examples of Arabic, Iranian and Mughal miniatures.

DECORATIVE ARTS
HIGHLIGHTS

Treasure of St-Denis; reliquary of St Thomas Becket Room 2

Descent from the Cross (ivory) Room 3

Tapestries, *Maximilian's Hunts* Room 19

Treasure of the Order of St-Esprit Rooms 27, 28

Crown Jewels Room 64

Madame Récamier's bedroom Room 67-73

The Apartments of Napoleon III Rooms 82-92

RICHELIEU FIRST FLOOR

MEDIEVAL PERIOD *Rooms 1-11* The earlier works in this section, from the Middle Ages (c 476 to the 16c), are made up mainly of small but exquisite pieces, including gold jewellery, reliquaries in finely wrought metal adorned with semi-precious stones, icons in mosaic, and carved ivory triptychs such as the *Barberini Triptych* (10c). The *Treasure of St-Denis* is a collection of superb ecclesiastical ornaments acquired in the 12c by Abbot Suger of St-Denis, including *Suger's Eagle*, an eagle-shaped antique porphyry vase mounted in silver gilt, and the rock crystal Vase of Eleanor of Aquitaine.

Other outstanding pieces are the enamel *Reliquary of St Francis of Assisi* (early 13c), the so-called *Ring of St Louis* (14c) from St-Denis, and the gold sceptre of Charles V with a statue of Charlemagne.

Later objects (15c-16c) tend to increase in size, ranging from an impressive collection of Hispano-Moorish lustreware to delightful medieval *millefleurs* tapestries, strewn with flowers and animals.

RENAISSANCE PERIOD *Rooms 12-33* The 16c marks the shift from religious to domestic items. Typical of the first half of the 16c, are painted enamels and furniture as well as the magnificent series of tapestries, *Maximilian's Hunts* (1531-3), which belonged to Louis

XIV. Smaller luxury French items include 16c-17c jewellery, clocks and watches, in enamel, gold and precious stones. From Italy are **Jean Boulogne**'s (Giambologna; 1529-1608) famous bronze, *Nessus carrying off Deianeira*. There are also religious treasures associated with the French Order of Chivalry of the Holy Spirit (St-Esprit), founded by Henri III in 1578. Rare examples of Renaissance furnishings are complemented by the rustic ceramics by **Bernard Palissy** (c 1510-89). The 17c saw the introduction of Ebénisterie (cabinet making) which revolutionized French furniture.

SULLY FIRST FLOOR

17C-18C *Rooms 34-36* These rooms feature the work of the excellent cabinet-maker **André-Charles Boulle** (1642-1732), at the time of Louis XIV, and small, decorative items of the 17c and 18c in ivory, tortoiseshell and amber, as well as tableware and wine glasses.

CERAMICS & FURNITURE *Rooms 36-62* Here are 18c French faience and porcelain, *boiseries* (panelling), and furniture and luxury items such as the *nécessaire* of Marie Leszczynska (1729), the Savonnerie carpet made for the Apollo Gallery (1667). Furniture representing the styles of Louis XV (1715-74) and Louis XVI (1774-91) includes Marie-Antoinette's flat-topped bureau by Hauré and G. Beneman (1787). In addition are Chinoiserie objects by Martin Carlin (c 1730-85) and a *toilette* in crystal and bronze which belonged to the Duchess of Berry.

CROWN JEWELS *Room 64* The Crown Jewels are housed here temporarily while the Apollo Gallery is being renovated. The glittering collection includes semi-precious vessels and individual objects, such Louis XV's crown (1722) - the gems were replaced by coloured stones after his coronation. Many were sold in 1887, but those that remain, such as the Regent diamond (137 carats) and the Côte de Bretagne ruby, later cut into the shape of a dragon as a decoration of the Order of the Golden Fleece.

RICHELIEU FIRST FLOOR

EMPIRE STYLE *Rooms 67-73* The most interesting piece is the
bedroom of Madame Récamier from the old Hôtel Necker. Her
trend-setting taste in interior design launched the Empire Style
and in the early 19c the house became one of the great sights of
Paris, especially the bedroom. Typical of Empire style objects are
the prestigious silver-gilt tea service (1810) and porcelain,
including the Sèvres porcelain coffee-service with views of Egypt
taken to St Helena by the Emperor; also monumental furniture
(1804-15) by Jacob-Desmalter.

JULY MONARCHY *Rooms 75-81* A reconstruction of the
bedchamber at the Tuileries occupied by Louis XVIII, then by
Charles X, and other works of the Restoration and July Monarchy
(1814-48) are representative of items encouraged by the Directoire
for the Exposition of 1819 designed to stimulate national
production and limit imports - especially from England.

RICHELIEU FIRST FLOOR

APARTMENTS OF NAPOLEON III *Rooms 82-92* These are a
curiosity for their ostentatious décor and furnishings, constituting
a unique ensemble of the period. They were created by Hector
Lefuel in 1857-61 to house the Ministry of State, and to link the
Tuileries Palace with the Louvre. After the fire in 1871, which
damaged this wing, the building was made over to the Ministry of
Finance, which remained there until the Grand Projet du Louvre
in 1989.

A series of antichambers leads to the main reception rooms in
sumptuous Louis XIV style. The Salon-théâtre has a charming
floral and musical decoration.

The large and magnificent Grand Salon, which glitters with gold,
is adorned with putti and draped in crimson velvet. The ceiling
painting by Charles-Raphaël Maréchal depicts the *Linking of the
Louvre and the Tuileries by Napoleon III*. The Small Dining Room is
more sedately decorated in sea-green marble and dark wood,
while the Large Dining Room has a painted ceiling.

GREEK, ETRUSCAN AND ROMAN ANTIQUITIES
HIGHLIGHTS

Pre-classical Greek, Cycladic art	Room 1
Borghese Gladiator	Room B
Venus de Milo	Room 12
Etruscan Sarcophagus of a Married Couple	Room 18
Treasure of the Boscoreale	Room 33
Winged Victory of Samothrace	Escalier Daru

GREEK ANTIQUITIES
DENON LOWER GROUND FLOOR

PRE-CLASSICAL GREECE *Rooms 1-3* Third to first millennium BC, with examples of Cycladic art and the large *Calyciform Crater* (vase) depicting the Combat of Hercules and Antaeus. Archaic Greek art, 7c-5c BC, produced the elegant and delicately modelled *Kore of Samos* (c 570-550 BC), one of the oldest and best authenticated works of island sculpture. The *Rampin Head* (6c BC) is a finely modelled piece, originally part of the statue of a horseman.

DENON GROUND FLOOR

SALLE DU MANÈGE *Room A* Former riding school of Napoleon III's new Louvre (1855-7). Coloured marbles and huge Albuni basins.

ROOM B Antique sculptures from royal and other major historic collections including the *Borghese Crater* (c 50 BC), and the *Borghese Gladiator*.

SULLY GROUND FLOOR

ROOMS 5-16 The **Rotunda of Mars** (1655-8) was the original entrance to the museum in 1809. In these rooms are fragments of the Parthenon frieze, the so-called Corridor of Pan and Praxiteles rooms with originals and antique replicas. The *Venus de Milo*

(Aphrodite) (Room 12), found in five fragments by a peasant in 1820 on the island of Melos in the Greek archipelago, is now regarded as a 2c BC copy after a 4c BC original.

ROOM 17 (off Room 8) The **Salle des Cariatides** is the oldest surviving room in the palace. Here are antique replicas of works from the 4c BC to the Hellenistic period (3c-1c BC): *Hermes Fastening his Sandal*, after the original of c 320 BC by Lysippos, and *Artemis the Huntress (Diana of Versailles)*, a Roman adaptation of a work of c 330 BC, acquired from Rome by François I.

Winged Victory of Samothrace (c 190 BC)

ETRUSCAN AND ROMAN ANTIQUITIES
DENON GROUND FLOOR

ROOMS 18-31 Etruscan work from Cerveteri, Italy, includes five terracotta plaques (c 530 BC), and the remarkable *terracotta sarcophagus* (c 520-510 BC) with the lifelike figures of a husband and wife reclining on a funeral couch. There are mosaics of *The Seasons* (c 325 AD) from a villa near Antioch, and a temple frieze depicting a battle between Greeks and Amazons (2c BC).

ESCALIER DARU On the monumental Escalier Daru (staircase) stands the *Winged Victory of Samothrace* (c 190 BC), one of the most celebrated pieces in the Louvre. Of Parian marble, this marvellous sculpture, found in 1863, originally stood on a terrace on the island of Samothrace in the Aegean. The figure seems to stand at the prow of a galley with wings spread, the draperies of her tunic clinging as if flattened by the wind. The right hand (displayed in a case nearby) discovered in 1950, suggests that it was raised to announce a naval victory, a clue to the date of the figure.

GREEK AND ROMAN ANTIQUITIES
SULLY FIRST FLOOR
ROOM 34 The Grand Cabinet du Roi Louis XIV (c 1660) contains some 100 pieces of Greek and Roman glass.

ROOMS 32-38 The antichamber ceiling was decorated by Braque in 1953 (restored 2002). Here are Greek and Roman bronzes and precious objects. The **Treasure of Boscoreale** features superbly decorated silver objects discovered in 1895 in a villa buried when Vesuvius erupted in AD 79. Other objects include a winged helmet encircled by a golden crown and the *Apollo of Piombino*, a 1c BC bronze figure, with copper encrustations, retrieved from the sea near Piombino, Italy.

ROOMS 39-47 contain a superlative group of some 2000 Greek vases and vessels (800-400 BC) arranged both chronologically and by decorative motifs.

EGYPTIAN ANTIQUITIES
HIGHLIGHTS

Akhethetep mastaba	Room 4
Mummy cases and sarcophagi	Room 14
Seated Scribe and *Stela of Nefertiabet*	Room 22
Statue of *Amenophis IV*	Room 25
Statue of the *God Amon with Tutankhamen*	Room 26
Reconstruction of the monastery church of Baouit	Room C

PHARAONIC EGYPT, THEMATIC CIRCUIT
SULLY GROUND FLOOR

CRYPT OF THE SPHINX *Rooms 1, 2* The large and majestic **Sphinx** of polished red granite dates to at least 1898-1866 BC. From here a staircase leads to a large kneeling statue of **Nakhthorheb** (c 595-589 BC), which symbolizes the permanence of the Egyptian civilization and the importance of religion.

DAILY LIFE IN ANCIENT EGYPT *Rooms 3-11* These are popular rooms which introduce Egypt through vivid presentations of everyday life starting with the Nile, source of life and fertility. The most fascinating exhibit is the limestone **Akhethetep mastaba** (a tomb), 2400 BC, with vivid scenes depicting the life of the defunct dignitary in his rural domain, including the master's banquet. Further displays include agriculture, cattle breeding, weights and measures, writing and the tools of the scribes as well as arts and crafts, and dwellings and furnishings. The theme of food is based on the Ideal Menu for the Dead, sculpted on the walls of a tomb of the Old Kingdom complete with the names of the delicacies. There are also musical instruments, and high-quality objects of adornment.

THE TEMPLE *Rooms 11-12bis* These rooms recreate the forecourt of the temple and the temple itself. On the approach, an enfilade of six limestone sphinxes forms a processional alley (*dromo*), and from the base of the obelisk of the Temple of Luxor are large, red granite *cynocephali* (baboons). Large sculptures and pieces of architecture evoke the temple and its courtyards covering 3000 years of Egyptian art, with the great deeds of the Pharaohs listed on the Wall of the Annales of King Thutmosis III. At the heart of the temple is the naos or chapel sheltering a statue of **Osiris**. Objects from the chapels include a large circular sandstone zodiac from the temple of Hathor at Dendera, showing the sky, planets and constellations in 50 BC.

CRYPT OF OSIRIS AND ROYAL TOMB *Room 13* (The Royal Tomb is downstairs.) Deceased kings were revered as gods and Egyptians believed that Osiris had reigned in the world before becoming sovereign of the dead. The approach to the magnificent pink granite *Sarcophagus of Rameses III* evokes the descent to the hypogeum of the Valley of the Kings.

MUMMIES *Rooms 14-19* A splendid display of wooden mummy cases along with stone sarcophagi and embalming and burial rites as well as objects from burial chambers showing the evolution in funerary customs over some 1000 years. Related displays are the over-25m papyrus *Book of the Dead of Hornedjitef*, and animals, sacred and mummified, associated with the gods such as Amon, Bastet, the cat-faced goddess of Bubastis and a magnificent statue of the *Bull Apis*.

PHARAONIC EGYPT, CHRONOLOGICAL CIRCUIT
SULLY FIRST FLOOR

On the north stairs leading to Room 20 is an illustrated chronology introducing this section.

ROOMS 20-21 The highlight of the **Nagada period** (c 4000-3100 BC) is a dagger from Gebel-el-Arak, with a hippopotamus-tooth handle carved with a battle scene. From the **Thinite period** (c 3100-2700 BC), the *Stela of King Zet Ouadji*, the Serpent King, has a particularly fine relief of a falcon, symbolizing the king, dominating a serpent enclosed in the walls of a fortress.

ROOMS 22-28 The **Old Kingdom** (c 2700-2200 BC) was the time of the great pyramids. The majority of the objects surviving from this period are funerary, and one of the most remarkable is the highly-coloured and intensely vibrant *Seated Scribe*, with eyes of white quartz and rock crystal, found at Saqqara. The painted stone *Stela of Nefertiabet* from Giza reflects the degree of refinement reached during this period.

The **Middle Kingdom** (c 2033-1710 BC) marks the classical period of Egyptian civilization when the kings re-united their kingdom which had been carved up by invaders. Among the outstanding statues is the elegant female *Libation Carrier*, carrying food and water to a departed soul, and remarkable portrait statues of *Sesostris III* and of his son, *Amenemhat III*. A small corridor contains the most beautiful stele of the time.

The **New Kingdom** spanned the period c 1550 to 1069 BC. The glorious age when gigantic temples such as Karnac and Luxor were built, c 1550-1353 BC, is represented by the statue of *Prince Iahmes* and the more sensual portraits of *King Amenophis III* and *Touy*.

The time of Akhenaton and Nefertiti (c 1353-1337 BC) left an outstanding artistic legacy. *Akhenaton* (Amenophis IV) built the huge open courtyard near Karnac, with huge sculptures in a revolutionary style. The huge *statue* from the Colossus bears an elongated head of the Akhenaton who reigned for about 15 years and was later held in loathing by his people. It was given to France in 1972 by the Egyptian government in thanks for saving the temples of Nubia. Some of the most beautiful smaller Egyptian pieces in the Louvre include a *torso*, probably of Queen Nefertiti, in red quartzite.

The period c 1337-1295 BC was the time of the boy king Tutankhamen (d. c 1327 BC), the short-lived successor of Akhenaton. *Tutankhamen* is represented as a small figure with the god *Amon*.

The reigns of Rameses and other New Kingdom Pharaohs (c 1295-1069 BC) are represented by ceramic decorations from the Palaces of Delta, including a very fine statuette of *Amon* and his wife *Mout*, a display devoted to Rameses II, gold rings, and the *Stela of the Goddess Qadech*.

ROOMS 29-30 The **Saite Period** was marked by Persian domination (c 1069-404 BC). It has left the finest Egyptian bronze in the Louvre, the statue of *Karomama 'Divine Worshipper of Amon'*, which is sumptuously decorated with inlays of gold and silver.

The art of the last Pharaohs of Egypt up to the time of Cleopatra (404-30 BC) bears witness to the presence of Hellenistic influences after 322 BC when Alexander the Great entered Egypt. Here is the abundantly decorated, gilded *cartonnage* from the *Coffin of Tacheretpaankh*.

ROMAN EGYPT AND COPTIC ART
DENON LOWER GROUND FLOOR

ROMAN PERIOD *Room A* Funerary objects in Egypt during the Roman period (1c-4c AD) consist of painted shrouds, mummies and decorated coffins, and objects which accompanied the deceased to the tomb. There are also Roman portraits on wood and masks painted in the ancient Egyptian tradition.

COPTIC ART, 3C-14C AD *Rooms B, C* show the influence first of Roman Egypt and, after the mid-7c Arab conquest, of aspects of Muslim art on sculptures, textiles, and metal and glass objects. The culmination of the Coptic section is the **Baouit Room**, with a display focussed around a reconstruction of part of the monastery church of Baouit, founded in the 4c-12c.

AFRICAN, ASIAN, OCEANIC AND AMERICAN ARTS
DENON GROUND FLOOR (EXTREME WEST)

Enter by Porte des Lions. This section contains key works belonging to a new museum planned for 2005 on Quai Branly. The artefacts are organized into four main cultural regions: Africa, Asia, Oceania (Pacific and Australia) and the Americas.

on route

Arc de Triomphe, pl du Général de Gaulle, 8th; daily April-Sept 9.30-23.00; Oct-March 10.00-22.30, closed 1/1, 1/5, 8/5 am, 14/7, 11/11 am, 25/12; *T* 01 55 37 73 77. Begun by Napoleon I, his funeral cortège passed under it in 1840. Observe the swirling traffic from the top. Tomb of the Unknown Soldier below. Colossal relief carvings on its faces.
M Charles-de-Gaulle-Étoile

Bibliothèque Nationale Richelieu, 58 rue de Richelieu, 2nd; Mon-Fri 13.00-17.45, Sat to 16.45, Sun and PH 12.00-18.00, closed Mon; *T* 01 53 79 53 79. The old National Library contains the **Musée des**

Médailles et Antiques and holds temporary exhibitions. *M* Pont-Neuf

Carrousel Arch, 1st. A reduced copy of an antique Roman arch by Percier and Fontaine built 1806-28 to commemorate Napoleon I's victories. *M* Palais-Royal-Louvre

Grand Palais, 3 av du General Eisenhower, 8th; open during exhibitions, daily 10.00-20.00; *T* 01 44 13 17 17. Built of glass, steel and stone in 1900 for the Exposition Universelle. *M* Champs-Élysées-Clémenceau, Franklin Roosevelt

Jardin des Tuileries, 1st. Named after medieval tile-kilns (*tuileries*), the gardens developed in the 16c. Spread over 32ha, it has two ponds, a wooded area, terraces and flower-beds, and sculptures. *M* Concorde, Tuileries

Jeu de Paume, 1 pl de la Concorde, 8th; Wed-Fri 12.00-19.00, Tues 12.00-21.30, Sat-Sun 10.00-19.00, closed Mon; *T* 01 47 03 12 50. Originally a real (royal) tennis court, the gallery, on the edge of the Jardin des Tuileries, is used for contemporary art exhibitions. *M* Concorde

La Madeleine, pl de la Madeleine, 8th; daily 7.30-19.00; *T* 01 44 51 69 00. Begun in 1806 by Napoleon I, this neo-Greco-Roman church creates a visual counterpart to the Assemblée Nationale across the Seine. *M* Madeleine

Musée d'Art Moderne de la Ville de Paris, 11 av du Président Wilson, 16th; Tues-Fri 10.00-17.45, Sat-Sun 10.00-18.45, closed Mon and PH; *T* 01 53 67 40 00. This important museum of 20c works belongs to the City of Paris. The permanent collection includes a number of Fauve and Cubist works, paintings by Robert Delaunay and Fernand Léger, and members of the School of Paris, as well as Dufy's mural, *La Fée Electricité* (1937). Frequent temporary exhibitions. Café. *M* Iéna, Alma-Marceau

Musée des Arts Décoratifs, 17 rue de Rivoli, 1st; Tues-Fri 11.00-18.00, Sat-Sun 10.00-18.00, closed Mon; *T* 01 44 55 57 50. Its collections include fashion and textiles, advertising material (posters, drawings, videos, etc) and decorative arts from the Middle Ages to the 19c. Attractively renovated. *M* Palais-Royal-Louvre

Musée Galliera de la Mode de la Ville de Paris, 10 av Pierre 1er de Serbie, 16th; during exhibitions 10.00-18.00, closed Mon; *T* 01 56 52 86 00. Temporary exhibitions of clothes and fashion. *M* Iéna, Alma-Marceau

Musée Guimet des Arts Asiatiques, 6 pl d'Iéna, 16th; 10.00-17.45, closed Tues; *T* 01 56 52 53 00. An outstanding collection of art and objects illustrating the diversity of cultures and civilizations in Asia. Café. *M* Iéna, Boissière

Musée Jacquemart-André, 158 blvd Haussmann, 8th; daily 10.00-18.00. *T* 01 45 62 11 59. Superb collection and charming setting, including

French 18c and Italian Renaissance art, in a former private house. Café. **M** Charles-de-Gaulle-Étoile

Musée Nissim de Camondo, 63 rue de Monceau, 8th; Tues-Sun 10.00-17.00, closed Mon; **T** 01 53 89 06 40. Rare collection of 18c furniture and objets d'arts in a recreated 18c setting. **M** Villiers, Monceau

Opéra Garnier, pl de l'Opéra, 9th, **T** 01 40 01 22 63. The lavish opera house (1861-75) designed by Charles Garnier. The public areas can be visited when not in use and there is a small **opera museum**; 10.00-17.00. **M** Opéra

Orangerie, pl de la Concorde, 1st. Closed for refurbishment until 2005. Best known for **Monet's** *Waterlillies* series (1927) and 144 Impressionist and early 20c works. **M** Concorde

Palais de l'Elysées, 8th. The heavily guarded official residence of the French President since 1873. Built in 1718, it stands between rue du Fbg St-Honoré and av de Marigny. **M** Franklin Roosevelt

Palais Royal, 1st. The former palace is now government offices, but the arcaded square and gardens is a pedestrian oasis with a modern fountain (1985-6) by Daniel Buren. **M** Palais-Royal-Louvre

Petit Palais, av Winston-Churchill, 8th. Built 1897-1900 to house the Musée des Beaux Arts de la Ville de Paris. Closed until 2005 for renovation. **M** Champs-Élysée-Clémenceau, Franklin-Roosevelt

Place de la Concorde, 8th. Historic site and great open square built 1757-75 between the Seine, the Champs Elysées and the Tuileries. Louis XVI was guillotined here in 1793. Its present appearance dates from 1852. The 13c BC Obelisk of Luxor in the centre was a gift from Egypt in 1836. **M** Concorde

Pont des Arts, a pedestrian bridge built of cast iron in 1801-3 (rebuilt 1983-5), named after the Palais des Arts, as the Louvre was then called. **M** Palais-Royal-Louvre

Pont Royal, spanning the Seine west of the Louvre was built 1685-9. The last pillar on either bank has a hydrographic scale indicating the low-water mark as well as various flood-marks. **M** Tuileries

Pont Solférino Millennium footbridge linking the Tuileries gardens and the Musée d'Orsay, designed by Marc Mimram. **M** Tuileries, **RER** Musée-d'Orsay

St-Germain l'Auxerrois, 2 pl du Louvre, 1st. Gothic church which was the Parish church of royalty. 16c stained glass. **M** Palais-Royal-Louvre

commercial galleries

Artcurial, 61 av Montaigne, 8th, *T* 01 42 99 16 16. An interesting place exhibiting a vast range of artworks (prints, sculpture, jewellery); also sells art books and holds auctions. *M* Franklin-Roosevelt

Bernheim Jeune, 53 rue du Faubourg St-Honoré, 8th, *T* 01 42 66 60 31. Well-established gallery whose artists include Belloni, Fontanarosa, Fulcrand, Humblot, Morgan-Snell. *M* Concorde, Miromesnil

Espace Cardin, 1 & 3 av Gabriel, 8th, *T* 01 42 66 17 30. Former Théâtres des Ambassadors taken over by Cardin in 1971 to show his collections, and used to promote new artistic talents of all kinds through temporary exhibitions. *M* Concorde

Jérome de Noirmont, 38 av Matignon, 8th, *T* 01 42 89 89 00, www.denoirmont.com. Temporary exhibitions of works by contemporary photographers. Also **Noirmont Prospect**, 5 rue Jean Mermoz, 8th. Promotes the work of young artists, sold at affordable prices. *M* Miromesnil, Franklin Roosevelt

Lelong, 13 rue de Téhéran, 8th, *T* 01 45 63 13 19. Mainstream 20c international artists. *M* Miromesnil

Opéra Gallery, 356 rue St-Honoré, 1st, *T* 01 42 96 39 00. Contemporary French (Combas, Mouly, Tobiasse) and moderns (Chagall to Miró). *M* Concorde

Tamenaga, 18 av Matignon, 8th, *T* 01 42 66 61 94, www.artnet.com. Works by European and Japanese artists, favours figurative neo-Impressionistic style; some abstract. *M* Franklin Roosevelt

eating and drinking

There are plenty of places to eat in the immediate area of the Louvre, but the gardens of the Palais Royal, a stone's throw away from the museum, offer a pleasant alternative, especially in summer, where restaurants of every category reside under the surrounding arcades and in small adjacent streets. Along rue St-Honoré you will find some of the newer, trendier restaurants such as Costes, and the place du Marché-St-Honoré, a large square dominated by Ricardo Bofill's modern construction, is lined with cheerful cafés and restaurants, several offering alfresco eating. If you are gasping for a good cuppa after a heavy day's shopping, a selection of sedate tea rooms and quirky shops with cafés can be found around rue Royale and place de la Madeleine.

AT THE MUSEUMS

LOUVRE

Under the pyramid, open to non-ticket holders:

- € **Café du Louvre**, in Halle Napoleon, bar and snacks.
- €€ **Restaurant du Grande Louvre**, *T* 01 40 20 53 41, is the smartest of the Louvre eating places, offering well-cooked dishes and reasonably-priced set menus.

Open to ticket holders only, Denon wing:

- € **Café Denon**, lower ground floor, light meals.

 Café Mollien, 1st floor, snacks.

 Café Richelieu, 1st floor, Richelieu wing, snacks and light meals.

MUSÉE JACQUEMART-ANDRÉ

- € **Café Jacquemart-André**, 158 blvd Haussmann, 8th, *T* 01 45 62 04 44; 11.30-17.30, closed Tues. Possibly the only place where you might take tea (or brunch or a light lunch) below a ceiling painted by Tiepolo. *M* Etoile-Charles-de-Gaulle

MUSÉE D'ART MODERNE DE LA VILLE DE PARIS

- € **La Terrasse**, 11 av. du Président Wilson, 16th, *T* 01 53 67 40 00. In season the teak terrace is open for light meals. *M* Charles-de-Gaulle-Étoile

MUSÉE GUIMET

- € **Maxence**, 6 pl d'Iéna, 16th, *T* 01 47 23 58 03. Restaurant on the ground floor serving snacks, salads, lunches. *M* Iéna, Alma-Marceau

SURROUNDING AREA

€ **Angelina's**, 226 rue de Rivoli, 1st, *T* 01 42 60 82 00. A smart tea room where you can indulge in a rich hot chocolate, or a *mont blanc* made from *crème de marron* and cream. *M* Tuileries

Bennett, 40 pl du Marché-St-Honoré, 1st, *T* 01 42 86 04 24. Reasonably priced so lunchtime is busy. *M* Tuileries, Opéra

Bernardaud, 11 rue Royale, 8th, *T* 01 47 42 82 66. Up-market tea salon and store selling innovative homeware. *M* Concorde, Madeleine

Cuisine & Confidences, 33 pl du Marché-St-Honoré, 1st, *T* 01 42 96 31 34; daily 8.00-19.00. Super selection of generous salads; Sunday brunch. *M* Tuileries, Opéra

Fauchon, 30 pl. de la Madeleine, 8th, *T* 01 47 42 90 10; Mon-Sat, 8.30-19.00. A *salon de thé* in the most elegant of grocery stores. *M* Madeleine

La Ferme Opéra, 55-57 rue St-Roch, 1st, *T* 01 40 20 12 12. Wide range of mainly vegetarian and organic self-service choices. *M* Opéra, Pyramides

Instant Délices, 21 rue St-Roch, 1st, *T* 01 42 60 90 29. Mon-Fri. Miniscule vegetarian restaurant with €18 menu. *M* Tuileries

Ladurée, 16 rue Royale, 8th, *T* 01 42 60 21 79. Established in 1890 this is *the* place to eat a macaroon and for a modest sum rub shoulders with Parisian chic. *M* Concorde, Madeleine

Lanvin, 22 rue du Fbg St-Honoré, 8th, *T* 01 44 71 33 33. In the basement is the fashionable **Café Bleu**, open Mon-Fri 12.00-18.00, Sat 12.00-15.00. *M* Concorde

Lavinia, 3-5 blvd de la Madeleine, 1st, *T* 01 42 97 20 20. Lunch and tapas are served upstairs in this extensive Spanish wine store. *M* Madeleine

Macéo, 15 rue des Petits-Champs, 1st, *T* 01 42 96 98 89. Modern cooking with some zingy twists to traditional dishes. The *prix fixe* are a good deal. Vegetarian dishes on offer. *M* Palais-Royal, Bourse

Muscade, 36 rue de Montpensier, 1st, *T* 01 42 97 51 36. A pleasant restaurant/*salon de thé* under the arcades of the Palais Royal. *M* Palais-Royal-Louvre

A Priori Thé, 35-37 Galerie Vivienne, 2nd, *T* 01 42 97 48 75; Mon-Sat 9.00-18.00. North of Palais-Royal, a lively lunch/tea shop in the elegant arcaded Galerie Vivienne. *M* Palais-Royal, Bourse

Le Rubis, 10 rue du Marché-St-Honoré, 1st, *T* 01 42 61 03 34. A rustic wine bar in which to enjoy a glass of Beaujolais with an *andouillet* (chitterlings sausage) or dish of the day. *M* Tuileries

Universal Resto - Le Food Court, Carrousel du Louvre, 99 rue de Rivoli, 1st, *T* 01 40 20 53 17. A wide choice of international food at the self-service on the mezzanine level. *M* Palais-Royal-Louvre

Verlet, 256 rue St-Honoré, 1st, *T* 01 42 60 67 39; closed Sun-Mon. The place to get a really good, strong *petit noir* coffee. *M* Tuileries, Concorde

€€ **L'Absinthe**, 2 pl du Marché-St-Honoré, 1st, *T* 01 49 26 90 04. Closed Sat midday/Sun. Typical Parisian bistrot with reliable 'home cooking', tending to classic with a modern touch. *M* Tuileries, Opéra

L'Ardoise, 28 rue du Mont-Thabor, 1st, *T* 01 42 96 28 18. Low-key setting leaves you to concentrate on the food which merits attention and is good value for money. *M* Concorde, Tuileries

L'Argenteuil, 9 rue d'Argenteuil, 1st, *T* 01 42 60 56 22. Tiny and contemporary, personal service and excellent cooking.
M Pyramides

Barlotti, 35 Tuileries/Opéra, 1st, *T* 01 44 86 97 97. A newish Italian restaurant in a spacious, bright setting. *M* Tuileries, Opéra

Bistrot St-Honoré, 10 rue Gomboust, 1st, *T* 01 2 61 77 78. A serious bistrot with friendly atmosphere and traditional dishes.
M Pyramides, Tuileries

Café Marly, 93 rue de Rivoli, Cour Napoleon, 1st, *T* 01 49 26 06 60. Very convenient for the Louvre. A Costes classic: laid-back, always bustling, reliable food, and a marvellous view of the Pyramid from the tables on the arcaded terrace. *M* Palais-Royal-Musée-du-Louvre

Café Ruc, 159 rue St-Honoré, 1st, *T* 01 42 60 97 54; daily 8.00-2.00. A trendy, chic Costes venture, with a range from club sandwiches to oysters and obscenely huge chocolate éclairs.
M Palais-Royal-Louvre

Il Cortile, 37 rue Cambon, 1st, *T* 01 44 58 45 67; closed Sat-Sun. Traditional Italian cooking served in three small rooms and an interior garden. Seriously good pasta; imaginative combinations, but never too complex. *M* Concorde, Madeleine

Le Dauphin, 167 rue St-Honoré, 1st, *T* 01 42 60 40 11. A well-established bistrot opposite the Comédie Française. Choices range from neo-classical to rustic southwest cuisine. *M* Palais-Royal-Louvre

Gaya, 17 rue Duphot, 1st, *T* 01 42 60 43 03; closed Sat–Sun. Concentrates on fish dishes, beautifully and simply cooked. Congenial surroundings and impeccable service. (Also 44 rue du Bac, 7th.) *M* Madeleine

Le Safran, 29 rue d'Argenteuil, 1st, *T* 01 42 61 25 30. Organic ingredients are used in this novel and intimate restaurant. The *menu surprise* might be just that; the *gigot de sept heures* (leg of lamb cooked for 7 hours) is reliably traditional. *M* Pyramides, Tuileries

Senso, 16 rue de la Trémoille, 8th, *T* 01 56 52 14 14. Terence Conran's latest venture in Pairs is an understated affair with good contemporary food. Lunch menu €25/€35. *M* Alma-Marceau

Le Soufflé, 36 rue du Mont-Thabor, 1st, *T* 01 42 60 27 19. A bit old-fashioned, but it's been serving light and airy soufflés for ever, both savoury or sweet varieties, including the classic *au Grand Marnier*; serves other, more solid food as well. *M* Concorde

€€€ Carré des Feuillants, 14 rue Castiglione, 1st, *T* 01 42 86 82 82; closed Sat–Sun. The south-western French origins of chef, Alain Dutournier, flavour but don't overwhelm the cuisine. Low-key elegance, superb fish dishes, and attention to detail account for its first-class reputation, but there is a price to pay. The lunch *prix fixe* is around €60. *M* Tuileries

Le Costes, Hôtel Costes, 239 rue St-Honoré, 1st, *T* 01 42 44 50 25. This ultra trendy Costes venture is decked out in excessive Napoleon III fashion and arranged around an Italian style patio. Probably chosen by its clientele as the place to be seen rather than for its culinary experience; the choice is limited, the portions small, but good quality; excellent *tarte chiboust* with lemon. *M* Tuileries, Opéra, Concorde

Le Grand Véfour, 17 rue de Beaujolais, 1st, *T* 01 42 96 56 27; Mon-Fri, 12.30-14.00, 20.00-22.00. If you want to push the boat out, this comes very high on the list for a special occasion. Stunning mirrored 18c setting (ensure a reservation in the main room), faultless service, and heavenly gourmet cuisine. *M* Palais-Royal

Palais Royal, 110 Gallery de Valois, 1st, 75001, *T* 01 40 20 00 27. Refined and discreet, favoured by local business people. The food is not cheap but quality is assured. The terrace stretches to the Palais-Royal gardens. *M* Palais-Royal-Louvre

BARS

Buddha Bar, 8 rue Boissy d'Anglas, 8th, *T* 01 53 05 90 00; Mon-Fri 12.00-2.00; disabled access. A trendy and expensive bar/restaurant for watching people who want to be watched. Exotic décor, ethnic music and Asian food. More affordable at midday. *M* Concorde

Colette Waterbar, 213 rue St-Honoré, 1st, *T* 01 55 35 33 90. Shop and eat combo with a slick café in the *sous-sol* carrying 80 different bottled waters. Food is mainly veggie and healthy.
M Tuileries, Pyramides

Le Defender, Hotel du Louvre, pl du Palais Royal, 1st, *T* 01 44 58 37 89; open until 1.00. Smart bar with music (Scottish or bossa nova!) on Wed. *M* Palais-Royal

Le Fumoir, 47 rue de l'Amiral-Coligny, 1st, *T* 01 42 92 00 24; 11.00-2.00. This combo of bar, restaurant and library with comfortable chairs is very modish and draws a sophisticated young clientele. Light, modern cuisine. *M* Louvre-Rivoli

Harry's New York Bar, 5 rue Danou, 2nd, *T* 01 42 61 71 14. Legendary, unchanging and reliable. *M* Opéra

Hemmingway Bar, Hôtel Ritz, 15 pl Vendôme, 1st, *T* 01 43 16 30 30. Glamorously cosy bar for exotic cocktails. *M* Madeleine

Nirvana, 3 av Matignon, 8th, *T* 01 53 89 18 91. New lounge-club/bar/restaurant, open 8.00 to 4.00. Aimed at the in-crowd, electro music; entry average €16. *M* Franklin Roosevelt

Willi's Wine Bar, 13 rue des Petits-Champs, 1st, *T* 01 42 61 05 09; closed Sun. Behind the Palais-Royal, a great wine bar with interesting food. Best value at lunchtime. *M* Bourse, Pyramides

shopping

Under the arches of the Palais Royal, and in the shopping arcades of galerie Vivienne, passage des Pavillons and galerie Véro-Dodat, are a multitude of interesting shops and boutiques. The Carrousel du Louvre, 99 rue de Rivoli, 1st, open every day including Sunday, is a smart place with numerous fashion accessory boutiques and the Ile de France information centre as well as a food mall. Enter via escalators from street level, from the métro, or from the Louvre's Hall Napoleon.

Galeries Lafayette

To run the gamut of classy boutiques from place du Palais-Royal to the Champs-Elysées, follow rue St-Honoré and rue du Faubourg St-Honoré culminating with *haute couture* houses on avenue Matignon. Along the way you pass close to place Vendôme, place de la Madeleine and rue Royale with yet more gorgeous goodies.

ACCESSORIES

Castelbajac Concept Store, 31 pl du Marché St-Honoré, 1st, *T* 01 42 60 41 55. Madly modern and funky accessories, clothes, household goods. *M* Tuileries

Colette, 213 rue St-Honoré, 1st, *T* 01 55 35 33 90. Trendiest of concept stores: Nars and Kiehl's products, designer clothing, shoes and books. See Bars. *M* Tuileries

Daniel Swarovski, 7 rue Royale, 8th, *T* 01 40 17 07 40. Accessories in crystal - bags and jewellery. *M* Concorde

Hermès, 24 rue du Fbg St-Honoré, 1st, *T* 01 40 17 47 17. Timeless silk squares, superb leather accessories, and perfume. *M* Concorde

Mina Poe, 19 rue Duphot, 1st, *T* 01 49 52 35 15. New shop for a Yugoslavian designer selling exclusively handmade and unique pieces including very colourful shawls and bags. *M* Madeleine

Philippe Model, 33 pl du Marché St-Honoré, 1st, *T* 01 42 96 89 02. Wild and wonderful hats. *M* Tuileries

Renaud Pellegrino, 14 rue du Fbg St-Honoré, 8th, *T* 01 42 65 35 52. Multi-colour range of classy French designer handbags and shoes. *M* Concorde

ANTIQUES

Louvre des Antiquaires, 2 pl du Palais-Royal, 1st, *T* 01 42 97 27 00, www.louvreantiquaires.com. Tues-Sat 11.00-19.00. A three-tier treasure trove with 250 dealers' stalls. *M* Palais-Royal-Louvre

Marché aux Timbres, at the end of av. Matignon, in the 8th, close to Rond Point des Champs-Élysées. Thur, Sat, Sun 9.00-19.00. Philatelists' paradise. *M* Franklin-Roosevelt

BOOKS

Brentano's, 37 av de l'Opéra, 2nd, *T* 01 42 61 52 50. The American bookstore; international press; travel and art books. *M* Pyramides, Opéra

Delamain, 155 rue St-Honoré, 1st, *T* 01 42 61 48 78. Wide selection of French books of all types; English novels in translation. *M* Palais-Royal-Louvre

Galignani, 224 rue de Rivoli, 1st, *T* 01 42 86 09 31. Anglo-American books with section on international fine art. *M* Tuileries

W.H. Smith, 248 rue de Rivoli, 1st, *T* 01 44 77 88 99. English bookshop, international newspapers and magazines. *M* Concorde

CLOTHES

Cerruti, 15 pl de la Madeleine, 8th, *T* 01 47 42 10 78. Clever Italian classics combine casual with sophistication; male version, 27 rue Royale. (Also rue de Grenelle, 7th.) *M* Madeleine

Chanel, 31 rue Cambon, 8th, *T* 01 42 86 28 00. Ineluctable style taken up by Kurt Largerfield. (Shoes 25 rue Royale, 8th.) *M* Concorde

Chloé, 54 rue du Fbg St-Honoré, 8th, *T* 01 44 94 33 00. In the forefront of young, trendy and sexy designs are the creations of Phoebe Philo, in place of Stella McCartney. *M* Concorde

Comme des Garçons, 54 rue du Fbg St-Honoré, 8th, *T* 01 53 30 27 27. Rei Kawakubo's cleverly cut and structured women's clothing; casual wear by Junya Watanabe; plus variety of gadgets. (Also rue Etienne Marcel, 2nd.) *M* Concorde

Didier Ludot, 20 & 24 galerie Montpensier, 1st, *T* 01 42 96 06 56 and 125 galerie de Valois, *T* 01 40 15 01 04. Vintage designer clothes - Chanel, Dior, etc. *M* Palais Royal-Louvre

Givenchy, 28 rue du Fbg St-Honoré, 8th, *T* 01 42 65 54 54. *Prêt-à-porter* women's fashions by successful Welsh designer, Julien Macdonald.

(Also 3 and 8 av George V, menswear, 56 rue François 1er, rue du Cherche-Midi, 6th.) **M** Concorde

Gucci, 21-23 rue Royale, 8th, **T** 56 69 80 80. Clothes and accessories for men and women by top designer Tom Ford. (Also av Montaigne, 8th.) **M** Concorde

John Galliano, 384 rue St-Honoré, 1st, **T** 01 55 35 40 40. Dior's designer presented in a new boutique. **M** Madeleine

Joseph, 277 rue St-Honoré, 1st, **T** 01 53 45 83 30. Chic clothes for men and women by Ettegui. **Joe's Café** is downstairs. **M** Tuileries

Lanvin, rue du Fbg St-Honoré, 8th, no. 15 for men, and no. 22, for women, **T** 01 44 71 33 33. Timeless elegance. See Eating and Drinking. **M** Concorde

Lolita Lempicka, 14 rue du Fbg St-Honoré, 8th, **T** 01 49 24 94 01. Luxurious setting for out-of-the-ordinary evening numbers; day dresses and shoes. **M** Concorde

Maria Luisa, 2 rue Cambon, 8th, **T** 01 47 03 96 15. One of four adjacent boutiques selling trendy designer fashions; no 4, shoes; 19bis and 38 rue du Mont-Thabor, men's fashions and sportswear. **M** Concorde

Marcel Marongiu, 203 rue St-Honoré, 1st, **T** 01 49 27 96 38. One of the most popular designers right now who manages successfully to blend sophistication and practicality. **M** Tuileries

Martin Margiela, 25bis rue Montpensier, 1st, **T** 01 40 15 07 55. Hidden under the Palais-Royal arcades, this Belgian fashion guru prefers an 'incognito' style in women's clothes. Men's at 23 passage Potier. **M** Palais Royal-Louvre

Nathalie Garçon, 15-17 galerie Vivienne, 2nd, **T** 01 40 20 14 00. Feminine clothes with lots of appeal and character in a friendly shop. **M** Pyramides, Bourse

Prada, 6 rue du Fbg St-Honoré, 8th, **T** 01 58 18 63 30. Fashion with an irresistible draw and cachet. (Also St-Germain, 6th.) **M** Concorde

Versace, 62 rue du Fbg St-Honoré, 8th, **T** 01 47 42 88 02. Emporium of men's and women's ready-to-wear, accessories, jewellery, etc. Setting somewhat over-the-top. **M** Concorde

DEPARTMENT STORES

Madelios, 23 blvd de la Madeleine, 1st, **T** 01 53 45 00 28, www.madelios.com. Tax free shopping for all top brand name fashions. Also has a café. **M** Madeleine

Galeries Lafayette, 40 blvd Haussman, 9th, *T* 01 42 82 34 56, www.galerieslafayette.com. One of the best-known and most elegant stores, with a huge range of women's wear and accessories, and a revamped menswear section. Restaurants; fashion shows Tues at 11.00, and Apr-Oct, Fri 14.30. *M* Chaussée-d'Antin, La Fayette

Le Printemps, 64 blvd Haussman, 9th, *T* 01 42 82 50 00, www.printemps.fr. Magnificent building, vast choice of perfumes, women's fashions, accessories, and jewellery. New menswear section on 6th floor. Café; fashion shows Tues & Fri at 10.00; open to 22.00 on Thur. (Also Centre Pompidou.) *M* Havre-Caumartin

DISCOUNT SHOPS (DÉGRIFFÉS)

Annexe des Créateurs, 19 rue Godot de Mauroy, 9th, *T* 01 42 65 46 40. Top labels discounted up to 70 per cent. *M* Madeleine, Auber

Boutique Stoclux, 8 pl Vendôme, 1st, *T* 01 49 27 09 31. New and used clothes by *grands couturiers* such as YSL, Prada, Chanel. *M* Tuileries

Haut de Gamme Stock, 9 rue Scribe, 9th, *T* 01 40 07 10 20, and 190 rue de Rivoli, 1st, *T* 01 42 96 97 47. Designer discount stores for men and women. *M* Opéra, Tuileries

FLOWERS

Les Fleurs, 110 rue St-Honoré, 8th, *T* 01 42 36 28 05. Mon-Sat 8.00-20.00, Sun 8.00-13.00. *M* Concorde

Marché aux fleurs, pl de la Madeleine, 8th. An outdoor flower market on the south side of the church. Mon-Sat 8.00-19.30. *M* Madeleine

FOOD

Debauve & Gallais, 33 rue Vivienne, 75001, *T* 01 45 48 54 67. Oldest chocolate maker in Paris. (Also rue des Sts-Pères, 7th.) *M* Bourse

Fauchon, 26 pl de la Madeleine, 8th, *T* 01 47 42 91 10. The most upmarket and exclusive of food stores where the window displays are an art in themselves. *M* Madeleine

Lavinia, 3-5 blvd de la Madeleine, 1st, *T* 01 42 97 20 20. New - a large Spanish-owned wine store; also French wines. *M* Madeleine

Toraya, 10 rue St-Florentin, 1st, *T* 01 42 60 13 00. Traditional Japanese pastries and tea salon. *M* Concorde

HOMES

Bernardaud, 11 rue Royale, 8th, *T* 01 47 42 82 66. Unusual, contemporary objects for the home as well as jewellery and a smart tea shop. *M* Madeleine

Pierre Frey, 22 rue Royale, 8th, *T* 01 49 26 04 77. Beautiful furnishing fabrics, soft furnishings, and other household goods. *M* Madeleine

Valombreuse, 108 rue du Fbg St-Honoré, 8th, *T* 01 47 42 79 19. Hand-embroidered linens and other lovely things. *M* Concorde

JEWELLERY

Place Vendôme 1st, *M* Tuileries. Many high-class jewellers are gathered in this square:

Alexandre Réze, no. 23, *T* 01 42 96 64 00. One-off unusual pieces made in the French workshops.

Chanel Joaillerie, no. 18. *T* 01 55 35 50 00.

Dior Joaillerie, no. 8, *T* 01 42 96 30 84. In a swish new boutique, original designs.

Fred, no. 7, *T* 01 42 86 60 60. Classic and contemporary pieces.

Jar, no. 7, *T* 01 42 96 33 66. Exclusive American designs.

Mauboussin, no. 20, *T* 01 44 55 10 00. Contemporary classics.

Alphee Bijoux, 8 rue St-Florentin, 1st, *T* 01 40 20 49 25. Attractive modern creations by la Fresange, Lempicka and Swarovski. *M* Concorde

M. Frey Wille, 9 rue de Castiglione, 1st, *T* 01 42 60 12 34. Viennese gold and enamel pieces. (Also rue St-Honoré, 1st.) *M* Concorde

KIDS

Bonpoint, 15 rue Royal, 8th, *T* 01 47 42 52 63. Very up-market kids' clothes, toddlers to teens. (Also 7th.) *M* Concorde

Marina, 82 rue du Fbg St-Honoré, 8th, *T* 01 42 65 96 21. Famous designers of such as Versace and Dior. Shoes at no. 84. *M* Concorde

Miki House, 366 rue St Honoré, *T* 01 40 20 90 98. Colourful, Japanese-designed children's wear. *M* Madeleine

Tartine et Chocolat, 105 rue du Fbg St-Honoré, 8th, *T* 01 45 62 44 04. Classic, elegant children's clothes. (Also St-Germain, 6th.) *M* Concorde

LINGERIE

Fifi Chachnil, 26 rue Cambon, 2nd, *T* 01 42 60 38 86. Pink, retro, frothy delights. *M* Concorde

La Perla, 20 rue du Fbg St-Honoré, 8th, *T* 01 43 12 33 60. Beautifully crafted in Italy, gorgeous, sexy and lacey; swim- and night-wear. (Also St-Germain, 6th.) *M* Concorde, Madeleine

MUSIC

Virgin Megastore, Carrousel du Louvre, 1st, *T* 01 44 50 03 10 (see above). Recorded-music emporium, books; café. (Also 52-60 av des Champs-Élysées, 8th.) *M* Palais-Royal-Louvre

PERFUME/BEAUTY

Anne Semonin, 108 rue du Fbg St-Honoré, 8th, *T* 01 42 66 24 22. Specialized beauty treatments including jet-lag massage. *M* St-Philippe-du-Roule

Salons du Palais Royal Shiseido, 142 galerie De Valois, 1st, *T* 01 48 27 09 09. Beautiful place, exclusive outlet for Serge Lutens' perfumes, great personalized gifts. *M* Palais-Royal

Stephane Marais, 217 rue St-Honoré, 8th, *T* 08 25 82 56 85. French designer's wide range of cosmetics and make-up techniques; lessons available. *M* Concorde

SHOES

Free-Lance, 416 rue St-Honoré, 8th, *T* 01 42 86 01 12. All kinds of good-quality, elegant and fashionable-funky footwear; beautifully made. (Also St-Germain, 6th.) *M* Concorde

Stephan Kelian, at 5 rue du Fbg St-Honoré, 8th (see also St-Germain). *M* Concorde

Tod's, 17 rue du Fbg St-Honoré, 8th, *T* 01 42 66 66 65. Casual, trendy. *M* Concorde

BEAUBOURG
MARAIS

Centre Pompidou

OPEN	Wed-Mon 11.00-22.00. Museum and exhibitions close 21.00. Atelier Brancusi 14.00-18.00
CLOSED	Tues, 1/5
CHARGES	€5.50; reduced price for 18-25-year-olds, €3.50. A day in the Centre, including exhibitions, €10; reduced price €8. Admission free, on presentation of valid proof of eligibility, for under 18s; recipients of certain social benefits (unemployed); disabled visitors. Free admission for all on the first Sun of each month
TELEPHONE	**01 44 78 12 33**; **01 44 78 12 33** (recorded)
WWW.	**centrepompidou.fr**
MAIN ENTRANCE	Place Georges Pompidou; other entrances rue St-Martin, rue du Renard, 4th
METRO	Rambuteau, Hôtel-de-Ville, **RER** Châtelet-les-Halles
DISABLED ACCESS	Rue du Renard or lifts from the Piazza to - Level 1. Reserved parking in auto park. **T 01 44 78 49 54**
AUDIO GUIDES	Available in English for the museum (€4.50) and for certain exhibitions
PUBLICATIONS	Free fold-out plan in English and bi-monthly publication of events (exhibitions, cinema, conferences, live performances). Museum Guide with selection of 150 masterpieces, €12
PHOTOGRAPHY	Hand-held cameras and camcorders may be used, without flash or tripods, to photograph works in the permanent collections except those marked with a red dot
SHOPS	Bookshops on Level 0, Level 4 and Level 6, with catalogues, postcards and posters. Novelty boutique on Level 1 has interesting designer articles, some based on Centre's collections
EATING	Non-ticket holders and disabled access to **Le Georges** restaurant on the 6th floor, with superb panoramas of Paris. The **Café** is on the mezzanine of the entrance hall

The Pompidou Centre is home to the French national collection of modern art, one of the most important in the world. Officially called the Centre National d'Art et de Culture Georges-Pompidou, it was conceived by the former President in 1969 as an interdisciplinary project comprising four departments: the DDC

which oversees the whole thing; Le Musée National d'Art Moderne/Centre de Création Industrielle (MNAM/CCI), the art collection; BPI, a multi-media free-access public library; and IRCAM, bringing together musical creation and technological research, housed in a separate building. It hosts activities such as dance, music, cinema and new technology. A new departure is the Carrefour de la Création, exploring technological innovation.

The ticket desks, Level 0, are opposite the main entrance and escalators, to the right of the entrance, whisk you up the exterior of the façade to the upper floors. Level 4 houses the Contemporary Collections (1960 onwards), and Level 5 the Historical or Modern Collections (1905-60). There is additional space on Levels 1 and 5 for temporary exhibitions.

THE BUILDING

The Pompidou Centre may not be the most loved but it is certainly one of the most controversial constructions since the Eiffel Tower.

Designed by an Anglo-Italian team of architects, Richard Rogers and Renzo Piano, it is a 15,000-ton metal box, 166m long, 60m wide, and 42m high with a glazed surface of 11,000 square metres. Functional elements such as air-conditioning and elevators, picked out in primary colours, are featured on the outside thus freeing up the maximum space inside. The seven floors (5 above ground) total 70,000 square metres.

The Centre was reborn in 2000 following a huge

Centre Pompidou

campaign of renovation and reorganization. More space has been
liberated on Levels 4 and 5 for the permanent collection so that
some 1500 works owned by the museum can be on display at any
one time.

   The piazza in front of the building has become a theatre space
for all kinds of street entertainment, bridging the gap between
the neighbourhood and the more formal events inside the Centre.

HIGHLIGHTS

Brancusi, *Sleeping Muse*   Level 5

Georges Braque, *Woman Playing a Guitar*

Robert Delaunay, *Joie de Vivre*

Henri Derain, *Two Barges*

Marcel Duchamp, *Fountain*

Max Ernst, *Ubu Imperator*

Henri Matisse, *Large Red Interior, The Sorrows of the King*

Pablo Picasso, *Woman in an Armchair, Harlequin*

Martial Raysse, *America, America*   Level 4

Joseph Beuys, *Homogenous Infiltration
for Grand Piano*

Jean Dubuffet, *Jardin d'hiver*

Yves Klein, *Monochrome Blue (IBK 3)*

Niki de Saint-Phalle, *The Bride*

Pierre Soulages, *Painting 1985, Polyptych C*

The Musée National d'Art Moderne/Centre de Création Industrielle
(MNAM/CCI) is made up of nine sections: Historical,
Contemporary, Graphic Arts, Photography, New Media, Art Films,
Architecture, Design and a Documentary section. One objective is
to show parallel developments in these fields and examples cover

most of 20c artistic creation. Only part of the Centre's large collection can be exhibited at one time so the selection and emphasis will vary from the description given here. The Historic Collections are rotated in the spring and the Contemporary in the autumn.

HISTORIC COLLECTIONS, LEVEL 5

The works are arranged chronologically overall, divided by artist, groups of artists, and by movement. The current hanging emphasizes recent acquisitions which include Braque's *Large Nude* (1908), Matisse's *Still Life with Chocolate Pot* (1900), *Seated Pink Nude* (1935), and *Lorette with a Cup of Coffee* (1917); Modigliani's *Portrait of Gaston Modot* (1918), and Picasso's *Young Woman with a Red Hat* (1921).

Some 200 works from André Breton's Surrealist collection have been acquired and include Dalí's *William Tell* (1930). The Centre has also received an important donation of works by Hantaï, and by Judit Reigl.

FAUVISM was the first great 20c movement, with its violent, impasto colour and contorted forms. Hedonistic in nature, it developed on the sunny Mediterranean and although short-lived as a movement it helped to liberate the palette of many artists. Those who painted in the Fauve style include Georges Braque, *L'Estaque* (c 1906) and *Small Bay at La Ciotat* (1907); Raoul Dufy, *Posters at Trouville* (1906); Maurice Vlaminck, *The Red Trees* (1906); also André-Derain, *The Two Barges* and *The Thames Embankment* (1905-6); Albert Marquet, *Matisse in his Studio* (1905), and Othon Friesz, *Portrait of Bernard Fleuret*. Georges Rouault, was a borderline Fauve - *Girl at the Mirror* (1906) - and became one of the few religious painters of the 20c - *La Sainte Face* (1933).

On no-one was the effect of the Fauve experience more emphatic and lasting than on **Henri Matisse**, illustrated in *Algerian Woman* (1909) and *Fish Bowl* (1914). The window was an important motif which ran throughout his career, as in *Window at Collioure*

CENTRE POMPIDOU
Levels -1 – 2

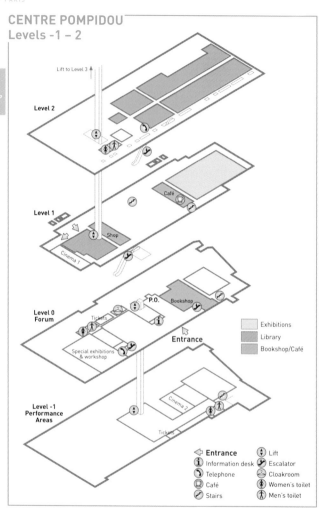

Entrance

Exhibitions
Library
Bookshop/Café

◇ **Entrance**
ⓘ Information desk
☏ Telephone
☕ Café
↗ Stairs

⊕ Lift
↗ Escalator
◠ Cloakroom
🚺 Women's toilet
🚹 Men's toilet

CENTRE POMPIDOU
Levels 3 – 6

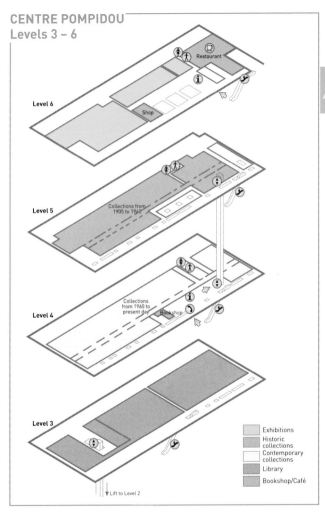

Level 6

Restaurant

Shop

Level 5

Collections from
1905 to 1960

Level 4

Collections
from 1960 to
present day

Bookshop

Level 3

Lift to Level 2

Exhibitions

Historic
collections

Contemporary
collections

Library

Bookshop/Café

(1914); another was the decorative Odalisques of 1925-6, and at times the two come together. In *Large Red Interior* (1948) he experimented further with the expressive qualities of colour learned from the Fauves, combined with simplified form.

Sculpture helped Matisse organize form, and among his bronzes are *Reclining Nude* (1907), *Jeanette I and IV* (1910-3) and *The Back I, II, III, IV* (1930). He used cut-outs later in his career as a technique for working directly with colour; examples of these include a copy of *Jazz* (Tériade edition, 1947), and *The Sorrow of the Kings* (1952).

CUBISM The creators of Cubism, both Analytical and Synthetic, were **Braque** and **Picasso**. The work of the two artists during this period demonstrates their parallel development. Compare Picasso's *Study for one of the Demoiselles d'Avignon* (1907), *The Guitar Player* (1910), *Woman Seated in an Armchair* (1910), with Braque's *Still Life with a Violin* (*Le Gueridon*) (1911), *Woman Playing a Guitar* (1913). Juan Gris was also a committed Cubist: *Breakfast* (1915). Among Cubist montages and sculptures are works by Henri Laurens, *The Bottle of Beaune* (1918), Raymond Duchamp-Villon, *The Horse* (1914-6), and Jacques Lipchitz, *Head of Gertrude Stein* (1920).

ORPHIC CUBISM was pioneered by **Robert Delaunay** whose interest in light and colour led to the first abstract works by a French painter: *Joie de Vivre* (1930) and *Rythme* (1934). His wife, Sonia Delaunay - *Electrical Prisms* (1914) - also embraced Orphism.

THE SCHOOL OF PARIS was a loose grouping of international artists such as **Amedeo Modigliani** (from Italy), Chaïm Soutine (from Russia), *The Groom* (1928), Foujita (from Japan), *My Interior* (*Still Life with Clock*), (1921), and Francis Gruber (from France); also Maria Elena Vieira da Silva (from Portugal), *The Library* (1949), and Antoni Tápies (from Spain). Another Russian, **Marc Chagall**, developed a very personal, poetic imagery with a few borrowings from Orphic Cubism: *To Russia the Donkeys and Others* (1911), *Death* (1908), *The Cemetery* (1917).

Juan Gris *Electric Lamp* (1925)

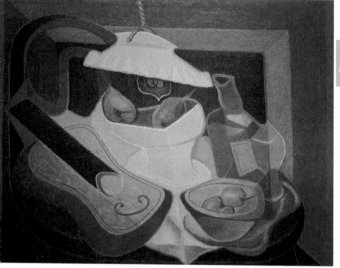

DADA was born in 1916 in Zurich out of the horrors of World War I. Anti-art, provocative and funny if sometimes obscene, it was taken up by Marcel Duchamp (see below), George Grosz, *Remember Uncle August, the Unhappy Inventor* (1919) and Kurt Schwitters, *Merz* (1926).

SURREALISM, which developed in the 1920s, was a synthesis of conscious and unconscious experience to create a new reality. Its roots were in Dada, literature, Freud's theories, and the hallucinatory paintings of **Giorgio di Chirico**, *Melancholy of an Afternoon* (1914). Its poet-painters, led by André Breton, had a far-reaching effect on all aspects of art. **Max Ernst**'s *Ubu Imperator* (1923), *Inner Vision* (1929), *Loplop Presents a Young Girl* (1930), engravings and collages; **Salvador Dali**'s *The Putrified Donkey* (1928) and **René Magritte**'s *The Double Secret* (1927).

Surrealism influenced such diverse artists as Hans Bellmer, *The Doll* (1934-7); Hans Arp, *Danseuse* (1925); Yves Tanguy; Roberto Matta, *Misdemeanours* (c 1941); Arshille Gorky and André Masson; Wilfredo Lam, *Light in the Forest* (1942); Victor Brauner, *Mr K's Powers of Concentration* (1934) and the sculptor Julio Gonzalez, *Woman doing her Hair* (1931). Francis Picabia embraced Cubism for a while - *Udnie* (1913) - before moving on to more aggressive anti-Salon-art tendencies as in *L'Oeil Cacodylate* (1921) and *Animal Trainer* (1923).

PABLO PICASSO The large group of works by Picasso cover most periods including the early period, *Portrait of a Young Girl* (1917), and his neoclassical production of the 1920s and 30s, such as *Girl reading* (1920), *Harlequin* (1923), and *Still Life with Antique Head* (1925). Surrealism featured briefly, as in *Figure* (c 1927) and *Minotaure* (1943). His mature works include grating female figures such as *Women with Pigeons* (1930) and the brightly coloured *Muse* (1935), while *Dawn Serenade* (1942) is an experiment with a variety of materials.

PIERRE BONNARD moved to the Côte d'Azur c 1925 to concentrate on interpreting form and light through colour, exemplified by his *Nude in the Bath* (1931), *Corner of the Table* (1935), *Studio with Mimosa* (1939-46), *Self Portrait in the mirror of a Bathroom Cabinet* (1945).

FERNAND LÉGER Briefly influenced by Delaunay and friends, *The Wedding* (c 1911) sought to reconcile art and science. He moved on to **Purism**, as in *Contraste de Formes* (1913), a rigorous, geometrically ordered form of Cubism introduced by Amédée Ozenfant and the architect Jeanneret (Le Corbusier). Following World War I, he returned to a figurative style, with monumental figures such as *Reading* (1924), *Composition with Three Figures* (1932) and *Composition with Two Parrots* (1935-9).

JOAN MIRÓ The poetic Catalan artist was profoundly influenced by Surrealism, shaping from it his own particular forms: *Interior,*

The Farmer's Wife (1922-3), *Siesta* and *The Catalan* (1925), and *Blue I, II and III* (1961) typical of his later works with floating, detached shapes on flat colour planes.

MARCEL DUCHAMP broke through the accepted boundaries of art with the enigmatic *Nine Malic Moulds* (part of *The Bride Stripped Bare by her Bachelors, even*) (1914-5), and especially *Fountain* (1917-64). This famous 'readymade' signed 'R. Mutt' was one of the most controversial works of the era and the jumping off point for future generations.

ABSTRACTION in fine and applied arts was born of the fertile breeding ground of the Bauhaus and cross-pollinated with movements throughout Europe, notably **De Stijl** in Holland and **Futurism** in Italy. The museum is rich in dynamic abstract works by Russian-born **Wassily Kandinsky**, such as *With the Black Bow* (1912) and *Yellow Red Blue* (1925).

PAUL KLEE Like Kandinsky, Klee was a member of the **Blaue Reiter** group in Munich and then of the Bauhaus (1922-33). Among his works are *Villas at Florence* (1926) and *Arrow in the Garden* (1929). **Constructivism**, described as hovering between utopia and integration, is represented by Antoine Pevsner, who produced finely balanced geometric works such as *Construction in Space* (1923-5) and *World* (1947), and the Ukranian, Kasimir Malevich, whose *Black Cross* (1915) influenced the Minimalists.

ITALIAN FUTURISM & DE STIJL Led by the poet and publicist Filippo Marinetti, this movement included Giacomo Balla, Umberto Boccioni and Russolo, *Dynamics of an automobile* (1911). Quite different were the De Stijl group of Dutch artists, associated with the magazine of the same name (1917-32), who produced pure abstraction: Theo van Doesburg, *Composition* (1918); **Piet Mondrian**, *Composition* (1937) and *New York City I* (1942); and Georges Vantongerloo, *S x R3* (1933-4).

EXPRESSIONISM The exaggerated forms and colour of Expressionism developed out of the pioneering work done by the Fauves in France and the Brücke and Blaue Reiter groups in northern Europe. Early exponents of Expressionism were Soutine, Kokoschka, Georges Rouault, Frantisek Kupka, *Vertical Planes I* (1912-3) and Ernst-Ludwig Kirchner, *La Toilette* (1913-20).

ART INFORMEL Art movements in France in the mid-20c included Art Informel, non-geometric abstraction of 1950s, practised by Jean Fautrier, *Hostage series* (1945), *The Skinned Boar* (1927), *The Tender Woman* (1946); Hans Hartung, and Nicolas de Staël *The Hard Life* (1946).

ART BRUT AND COBRA The main exponent of Art Brut was **Jean Dubuffet**, whose dark, primitive, graffiti-like works include *Dhôtel Tinted in Apricot* (1947) and *Metafisyx* (1950). Cobra, a group of northern painters, including Pierre Alechinsky, Karel Appel and Bram Van Velde, focused on unconscious, spontaneous creation.

SCULPTURE

From the period immediately preceding World War I are works by the brilliant young sculptor **Henri Gaudier-Brzeska**. **Constantin Brancusi** reacted against the emotional works of Rodin to create simplified, coherent shapes, as in *Sleeping Muse* (1910). (See the Brancusi Studio below.)

Alexander Calder, spurred on after a meeting with Mondrian, and closely associated with Miró, bent wire into witty sculptures, for example *Josephine Baker* (1926). He went on to make delicate mobiles: *White Disk, Black Disk* (1940-1) and *Mobile on Two Planes* (c 1955).

The sometimes chilling earlier works of **Alberto Giacometti** include *Suspended Ball* (1930), *Sharp Point in the Eye* (1931), *Woman with her Throat Cut* (1932-3) and *Unpleasant Object To Throw* (1931). More characteristic are the pared down, skeletal figures, *Seated*

Woman and *Venetian Woman V* (1956). **Germaine Richier**, one of France's great 20c sculptors, was influenced by Giacometti and Marino Marini and described as Existentialist. An example of her work is *The Storm* (1947-8).

On the exterior terraces are monumental sculptures by Henri Laurens, *Large Bather* (1947), Joan Miró and Alexander Calder.

PHOTOGRAPHY

The Pompidou Centre has a rich collection of some 12,000 prints, considered a vital document in the history of photography, including images by Man-Ray, Dora Maar, Brassaï and Lászlo Moholy-Nagy.

ARCHITECTURE AND DESIGN

Displays using drawings, models, furniture and other objects present designs ranging from Russian villages to the work of Le Corbusier, Jean Prouvé and Robert Mallet-Stevens as well as theoretical projects from De Stijl. Jean Prouvé trained as a structural engineer, and focused on pre-fabricated buildings; **Le Corbusier** was the most influential architect of his day, yet heavily criticized for his functional, flat-roofed designs.

The influence of the Bauhaus and De Stijl is obvious in furniture designs, notably Marcel Breuer's armchair *Club 33* (1925), and the resolutely progressive ideas of the Union of Modern Artists, Pierre Jeanneret and Alvar Aalto (Finland).

CONTEMPORARY COLLECTIONS, LEVEL 4

These displays cover the period from 1960 onwards and include painting, sculpture, casting, photomontage, photography, video, drawing, recycling, performance art, kinetic art, etc.

Large, playful fantasies which focus the mind and set the tone for the collections are works such as the mechanized sculpture by

Jean Tinguely, *Requiem for a Dead Leaf* (1970), Claes Oldenburg's rather threatening *Giant Ice Bag* (1969-70) and Ben's (Ben Vautier) *Magasin* (1958-73), a monumental montage of disparate objects making a Dadaistic anti-art statement. **Niki de Saint-Phalle**, *The Bride* (1963), was influenced by Art Brut and by Tinguely (with whom she designed the fountains in place Stravinsky next to the Centre) and Klein. Her assemblages are an extraordinary and often humorous comment on life.

OP ART, KINETIC ART AND GEOMETRIC ABSTRACTION, hard-edged works, optical or otherwise, began with **Joseph Albers**, *Hommage to the Square* (1956), and were developed by the great master of optical illusion **Victor Vasarély**, *Hô II* (1948-52) and *Procion, neg* (1957). Other artists in this group are Jesús Rafael Soto, *Rotation* (1952), and Yacov Agam, *Interior of the ante-room to private apartments of the Elysées Palace* (1972-4), an unsettling design for former President, George Pompidou.

NOUVEAU RÉALISME Founded in Paris in 1960 by **Yves Klein**, Nouveau Réalisme was a new perception of reality, re-interpreting the ready-mades of Marcel Duchamp. Among the Nouveaux Réalistes artists were Arman whose *Home Sweet Home*, an 'accumulation' of rubbish, is a criticism of 20c consumerism. Other proponents featured here are François Dufrêne, Daniel Spoerri, Mimmo Rotella and Gérard Deschamps. **Martial Raysse** moved on from Nouveau Réalisme to become a brilliant exponent of **European Pop**, demonstrated in *America, America*, a huge neon-lighted metal hand and *Made in Japan*, *La Grande Odalisque* (both 1964).

POP ART The museum's wide selection of Pop Art, which developed in England and the USA in the 1960s, includes **Andy Warhol**'s *Ten Lizes* (1963), Claes Oldenburg's *Ghost Drum Set* (1972), Robert Rauschenberg's *Oracle* (1962), Christo's *Package and Wrapped Floor* (1968), and James Rosenquist's *President Elect* (1960-1).

YVES KLEIN is associated mainly with the monochromatic works in a deep ultramarine that he patented as IKB. He believed that blue has no tangible reality and that by painting in monochrome colour is deprived of subjective associations. Between 1955 and 1962, he produced 194 IKBs, for example, on canvas *Monochrome Blue (IBK 3)* (1960) and an assemblage/sculpture *Tree - Large Blue Sponge* (1962). He used 'human brushes' to create such works as *Big Blue Anthropophagy, Homage to Tennessee Williams* (1960).

COMPRESSIONS AND DÉCOLLAGES César specialized in Compressions (of discarded objects), prompted initially by a lack of money: *Compression 'Ricard'* (1962). He later moved on to Expansions. Raymond Hains and Jacques de la Villeglé worked together making inventive *décollages* from peeled and torn up posters, such as *Ach Alma Manetro* (1949).

An important artist of the 20c, associated with the **Fluxus group** which was influenced by shamanism, was **Joseph Beuys**. *Homogenous Infiltration for Grand Piano* (1966) is a felt-wrapped grand piano - reminiscent of a rhinoceros - and *Skin* (c 1980) is the felt that was discarded when the artist changed the wrapping. Other members of Fluxus were Ben, Robert Filliou and Erik Dietman.

ABSTRACT EXPRESSIONISTS in France are headed by **Pierre Soulages**, the grand old man of French abstract painting who has remained constant to the possibilities of black, or black on white, on huge canvases, with designs which trace a form in space. The works depend on paint textures and the absorption or reflection of light, for example *All-black Peinture* (1979). The objectivity of titles such as *Painting 1985, 324 x 362 cm*, *Polyptych C*, deliberately avoids any figurative reference. **Conceptual Art**, the art of ideas which began with Marcel Duchamp, gave its name to a wide-ranging movement in the 1960s. One example of this is Joseph Kosuth's *One Colour, Five Adjectives* (1966), whereas the lyrical work of concept artist Simon Hantaï, *Without Title* (1969), is closer to Abstract Expressionism.

The USA is well represented by artists such as **Jackson Pollock** whose drip technique produced *'Number 26 A', Black and White*, **Mark Rothko** painted modern icons: *No 14 (Browns over Dark)* (1963). **Barnett Newman** was an initiator of Colour Field painting: *Shining Forth (to George)* (1961), *Jericho* (1968-9). There is also work by **Frank Stella**, *Parzeczew II* (1971), and **Willem de Kooning**, *Woman* (c 1952).

Other US artists whose work may be on view are **Jasper Johns**, *Figure 5* (1960), Alain Jacquet, *Le Déjeuner sur l'Herbe*, Ellsworth Kelly, Richard Lidner and Jim Dine.

A major figurative painter of the post-war period is **Francis Bacon**: *Van Gogh in a Landscape* (1957) and *Three People in a Room* (1964).

ARTE POVERA is an Italian expression which appeared in 1967 and means impoverished art. It aims to confront the materialism of the established art world by employing the most simple and worthless of materials. The main artists in this group are **Giuseppe Penone**, *Breath 6* (1978), *Albero*, and *Soffio 6*; **Mario Merz**, *Giap's Igloo* (1968), made of plastic bags filled with earth, and *Che fare*; and Jannis Kounellis, *Sans titre*. **Antiforme** is a sub-group of Arte Povera, whose temporary forms and 'soft non-fixed sculptures' were developed in the work of Eva Hesse's *Seven Poles* (1970), Robert Morris's curious yet eloquent felt *Wall Hanging* (1969-70) and Richard Serra's *Plinths* (1967).

INSTALLATIONS AND SPECIAL WORKS (1960-80) Considerable space is needed for these works, some of which are disturbing, others funny or puzzling, while focusing on 'representation'. **Jean Dubuffet**'s *Jardin d'hiver* (1968-70) is an unstable, black and white and disorientating monochromatic 'environment'. Jacques Monory's *Narrative Figuration* is a series using photos and film. Other works include Dorothea Tanning's *Chambre 202/Hôtel du Pavot* (1970), Edward Kienholz's *While Visions of Sugar Plums Danced in their Heads* (1964), Annette Messager's *The Pensioners* (1971-2), a series of vitrines, and *Pikes* (1992-3) an oblique feminist statement; Christian Boltanski's *A Fictive Autobiography*, a new type of storytelling and *The C.B. Archives* (1965-88, 1989) is a wall of 600 metal boxes containing the artist's life story.

SUPPORTS/SURFACES GROUP The period 1970-90 was a time of crisis, questioning and reaffirmation, represented in France by the Supports/Surfaces group. Typical are Daniel Buren's striped installations of *Cabin No 6: Draughtboards* (1985) and *Jamais Deux Fois la Même* (1967-2000). You might also see Toni Grand's, *Double Column* (1982), in wood and laminate, and Claude Rutault's *Toiles à l'unité* (1973) and *Légendes* (1985); others include Malcolm Morley and Georg Baselitz.

Works from 1990 to the present include series of large works, installations and techniques of casting, sculpture, photography, and video by artists such as Claude Closky, Patrick Tosani, Mona Hatoum, Marie-Ange Guilleminot and Gilles Barbier, Andreas Gursky and Pierre Huyghe.

ARCHITECTURE AND DESIGN

Megastructures and utopias as well as Pop Art designs are characteristic of the 1960s. Representative of the period 1970-80 are French architects **Christian de Portzamparc**, **Jean Nouvel**, the British **Norman Foster**, **Richard Rogers**, and the American **Frank Gehry**, plus designers **Gaetano Pesce** and **Martin Sezakely**. Architecture in the 1990s features the work of Dominique Perrault (Bibliothèque National Mitterand), Jean Nouvel (Institut Arabe), Rem Koolhaas, Toyo Ito and designers Philippe Starck, Ron Arad, Marc Newson, and Jonathan Ive.

ATELIER BRANCUSI

On the north of the Piazza Beaubourg the Atelier Brancusi, a small but dignified haven of monumental sculptures, should not be missed. The four studios of Constantin Brancusi's workshop have been exactly reconstructed, complete with works such as *Le Coq* (1935), as well as models, plinths, etc, plus photographs and other memorabilia. Visitors are able to circulate around the exterior of the studios to view them from different angles.

Musée Picasso

OPEN	1 April-30 Sept 9.30-18.00, 1 Oct-31 March 9.30-17.30
CLOSED	Tues, 1/1, 25/12
CHARGES	€5.50; reduced price for 18-25-year-olds, and Sun, €4. Combined with temporary exhibitions, €6.70; reduced price €5.20. Free admission for under 18s
TELEPHONE	**01 42 71 25 21; 01 42 71 25 21** (recorded)
WWW.	**musee-picasso.fr**
MAIN ENTRANCE	Hôtel Salé, 5 rue de Thorigny, 3rd
METRO	St-Paul, St-Sébastien Froissart, Chemin Vert
DISABLED ACCESS	The museum is accessible to disabled visitors and facilities include the loan of wheelchairs
PUBLICATIONS	*Guide du Musée Picasso*, €12.50; *Musée Picasso, les Chefs-d'oeuvre*, €19.50; *Petit guide to the Musée Picasso - Collections*, €2.90; *Petit Guide to the Hôtel Salé* (all available in English)
PHOTOGRAPHY	Hand-held cameras may be used to photograph works in the permanent collections, but no flash or tripods

Pablo Picasso bequeathed his collection to the State in lieu of death duties and the museum, which opened in 1985, exhibits a choice selection of works by the master himself as well as by other artists whose work he had collected. The collection is arranged as a progression through Picasso's artistic evolution, from 1894 to 1972. Housed in the beautiful Hôtel Salé, this is a favourite place to visit for admirers of modern art and fine buildings.

THE BUILDING

The Hôtel Salé (from *sel*, salt), one of the finest mansions in the Marais, was built between 1656 and 1659 by Pierre Aubert de Fontenay, a rich salt tax collector. After his death, the building was rented to the Venetian Embassy, and then a variety of educational institutions, among whose students in 1815 was the young Balzac. By 1964 it had become very run down, and the City of Paris purchased the hôtel, leasing it to the State who carried out a vast programme of renovation between 1974 and 1980, successfully transforming the mansion into a museum.

Arranged around a large courtyard, the building's original features have been preserved alongside modern exhibition spaces, and a majestic 17c staircase sweeps you up to the collections.

HIGHLIGHTS
Self-portraits, 1901 and 1906

Still life with Chair Caning

Man with a Mandolin and *Man with a Guitar*

The Pipes of Pan

Large Nude in a Red Armchair

Bull's Head (sculpture)

Portraits of Dora Maar and *Marie-Thérèse*

BLUE PERIOD *Rooms 1-3* A haunting *Self-portrait* (1901) painted when Picasso was 20; and *Celestina* (1904). Between the Blue and Rose periods he painted *The Two Brothers* (summer 1906). *Self-Portrait* (autumn 1906) shows the change of direction after his discovery of Iberian art, the culmination of which was *Les Demoiselles d'Avignon* (1906-7; MoMA, New York), for which the Museum has some preparatory works.

CUBISM (1907-15) *Room 4* *Still life with Chair Caning* (1912), his first collage, made with rope and printed oil-cloth; a three-dimensional interpretation *Sculpted Female Head of Fernande Olivier*; the witty construction *Violin* (1915). In total contrast is the 'Ingresque' *Portrait of Olga Khoklova seated* (1917), the Russian dancer who became his wife in 1918. Two representative paintings of the Cubist period are *Man with a Mandolin* and *Man with a Guitar*. both of 1911.

PAINTINGS BY OTHER ARTISTS IN THE COLLECTION *Room 5* These include Miró, *Self-portrait*; Balthus, *The Children*; Cézanne,

Five Bathers (1877-88), *Château Noir* and *Sea at l'Estaque*; Braque, *Guitar* (1913) and *Still Life with Bottle* (1910-1); Matisse, *Still Life with Oranges* (1912); Rousseau, *Self-Portrait with Lamp* and *The Artist's Wife*, plus works by Corot, Balthazar, and Modigliani.

'RETURN TO ORDER' OR CLASSICAL PERIOD *Rooms 6 and 6bis*
For Picasso this was the reappearance of an earlier (1905-6) stylistic trend within a universal avant-garde search for reassurance in long-term traditions after the chaos of World War I. *Bathers* (1918) recalls summer by the sea, first at Biarritz and later at Dinard, in the small-scale but effectively monumental *Women Running along a Beach* (1922); the *Village Dance* (1922), in pastel, has a timeless quality as does the sculptural *The Pipes of Pan* (1923). *Paul as a Harlequin* (1924) is his small son in fancy dress.

SURREALISM AND SCULPTURE, 1925-35 *Rooms 7-9* Although never part of the Surrealist group, its influence plus the impact of Picasso's personal problems at the time emerge in the aggression of *The Kiss* (1925), *Large Nude in a Red Armchair* (1929), *Figures by the Sea* (1931) and the sculpture *Metamorphosis II* (1928). The rounded forms of sculptures made at Boisgeloup are repeated in his paintings *Woman in Red Armchair* (1932) and *Nude in a Garden* (1934).

PICASSO AND THE MINOTAUR AND CHRISTIAN MYTH *Room 10* Drawings after Grünewald's *Isenheim altarpiece* of c 1516 paved the way for the violent *Crucifixion* (1930). Themes of the bull fight and the Minotaur recur frequently in Picasso's work. *Minotauromachie* (1930) mixes these opposing forces.

ROOM 11 *Women at their Toilette* (1838) is a huge collage of printed wallpapers, intended as a tapestry cartoon.

BRONZES, TERRACOTTAS AND CERAMICS *Rooms 12 and 14* Witty pieces such as the *Flute Payers* (1958), and *Woman with a Rush Chair* (1950). Examples of Picasso's ingenuity in reshaping ceramics made at Vallauris in the south of France include *Vase: Woman with a Mantilla* (1949).

THE GUERNICA PERIOD *Room 13* To express the horror of the bombardment of the Spanish Basque town, Picasso painted *Guernica* (1937, Madrid), for the Spanish Pavilion of the International Exhibition of that year. Two preparatory studies of *The Weeping Woman* are in this room. Towards the end of the 1930s Picasso's favours shifted from Marie-Thérèse Walter to the new focus of his life, Dora Maar. Both women are represented by portraits of 1937.

WAR AND LIBERATION *Rooms 15-16* During the war period, Picasso assembled and sculpted. Animals and birds always played an important role in his work, as in the cryptic *Bull's Head* (1942) created from an old bicycle saddle and handlebars, but his political anguish is reflected in *Cat with a Bird* (1938). *Massacre in Korea* (1951), after Goya, is a shockingly realistic image.

1950S' BOOK ILLUSTRATIONS AND OTHER WORKS *Room 17-18* *Reclining Female Nude* (1955) and the original plaster of *Baboon and its Baby* (1951), assembled from an assortment of objects including toy cars. *Nude Pregnant Woman* (1949) inspired by the birth of his two children with Françoise Gilot.

VALLAURIS TO VAUVENARGUES 1947-63 *Room 19* In 1945 Picasso met Jacqueline Roque, who became his wife in 1961. They lived in Provence at Vauvenargues of which *Dresser at Vauvenargues* (1959-60) is a souvenir. In *Déjeuner sur L'Herbe* (1960), the painter makes a burlesque tribute to Manet.

LATE PAINTINGS 1963-73 *Room 20* These remarkably vigorous and optimistic works, using colourful blues and oranges, include *Old Man Seated* (1970), *The Embrace* (1970), and *Seated Girl* (1970).

on route

Musée Carnavalet *Louis XIV*

Hôtel Carnavalet, 23 rue de Sévigné/Francs-Bourgeois, 3rd. A grand mansion of the Marais, built in 1548 and altered 1660, the courtyard has statues by Jean Goujon. It houses the very important collections of the **Musée Carnavalet**, which present the history of Paris through paintings, furniture, and memorabilia. Particularly striking are the reconstructed interiors saved from 17c and 18c Parisian mansions. 10.00-17.40, closed Mon and some PH; *T* 01 42 72 21 13. *M* St-Paul, Chemin-Vert

Hôtel de Soubise, 60 rue des Francs-Bourgeois, 3rd. Built 1705-12, the sumptuous Rococo interior (1712-45), with decorations by Boucher, was protected by the installation of the National Archives. Also home to the **Musée de l'Histoire de France** which holds frequent temporary exhibitions. Mon-Fri 10.00-17.45, Sat-Sun 13.45-17.45, closed Tues; *T* 01 42 27 60 96. *M* Hôtel-de-Ville, Rambuteau

Hôtel de Sully, 62 rue St-Antoine, 1st; courtyards open, bookshop Tues-Sun; *T* 01 44 61 21 69/01 44 61 21 70. Mansion with two courtyards, built 1624-30, for Sully, Henri IV's minister. It is now occupied by the Caisse National des Monuments Historiques. *M* St-Paul

Hôtel de Ville, pl de l'Hôtel de Ville, 4th, *T* 01 42 76 50 49. The City Hall (*Mairie*) of Paris, site of many historic events. This building (1874-84) is a picturesque replica of its 16c predecessor burned down in 1871. Group visits only. *M* Hôtel-de-Ville

Maison Européenne de la Photographie, 5-7 rue de Fourcy, 4th; 11.00-20.00, closed Mon, Tues and PH; *T* 01 44 78 75 00. Exhibition centre for photography in an 18c mansion. *M* St-Paul

Maison de Victor Hugo, 6 pl des Vosges, 4th; 10.00-17.40, closed Tues and PH; *T* 01 42 72 10 16. Home of the writer, 1832-48. Drawings by Hugo, furniture and memorabilia. *M* St-Paul

Musée d'Art et d'Histoire du Judaïsme, 71 rue du Temple, 3rd; 11.00-18.00, Sun 10.00-18.00, closed Sat; *T* 01 53 01 86 60. Located in the Hôtel St-Aignan, the collection traces the history of Jewish communities in France and West and North Africa through their culture and art. *M* Rambuteau

Musée des Arts et Métiers, 60 rue Réamur, 3rd; 10.00-18.00, Thur 10.00-21.30, closed Mon and PH; *T* 01 53 01 82 00. Dedicated to technical innovation, science and technology, from astrolabes to aeronautics, in the former abbey of St-Martin-des-Champs. *M* Arts-et-Métiers

Musée de la Chasse et Nature, 60 rue des Archives, 3rd; 11.00-18.00, closed Mon and PH; *T* 01 53 01 92 40. Art and objects appertaining to hunting and nature in a 17c *hôtel particulier* (town house) by François Mansart. *M* St-Paul

Musée Cognac-Jay, 8 rue Elzévir, 3rd; 10.00-17.40, closed Mon and PH; *T* 01 40 2707 21. Intimate museum of 18c art and furniture exquisitely presented in the Hôtel Donon of the same period; works by Boucher, Chardin, etc. *M* St-Paul

Musée de la Poupée, Impasse Berthaud, 3rd; 10.00-18.00, closed Mon and PH; *T* 01 42 72 73 11. A collection of over 500 French dolls and related accessories and toys, dating from 1800-2000. *M* Rambuteau

Opéra Bastille, 120 rue de Lyon, 12th; guided visits only; *T* 01 40 01 19 70. The shiny white face of the national opera house designed by Carlos Ott, which opened in 1989, overlooks Place de la Bastille. *M* Bastille

Pavillon de l'Arsenal, 21 blvd Morland, 4th; Tues-Sat 10.30-18.30, Sun 11.00-19.00, closed Mon, 1/1; *T* 01 42 76 33 97. Information, documentation and exhibitions in connection with City of Paris urban planning and architecture. *M* Sully-Morland

Place de la Bastille, 12th. Laid out in 1803 on the site of the fortress-prison attacked on the 14 July, 1789 at the Revolution. The July Column is a memorial to the 1830 Revolution. *M* Bastille

Place du Châtelet, 1st. Busy square on the banks of the Seine, on the site of an ancient fortified gateway, with two theatres and a fountain. *M* Châtelet

Place de l'Hôtel de Ville, 4th. Large pedestrianized square called place de Grève until the working-class uprising of 1830. It was, and still is, the scene of large gatherings, and French strikers are called *grévistes*. However, no longer the site of public executions. *M* Hôtel-de-Ville

Place des Vosges, 1st. A charming square built in the 16c/17c, with brick façades and shopping arcades surrounding public gardens planted with trees in 1783; an early example of town planning. *M* St-Paul

St-Eustache, 1st. Built 1532-c 1637, combining Gothic and Renaissance elements. Strong musical associations and important organ. Tomb of Colbert designed by Le Brun and statues by Coysevox, *Martyrdom of St Eustace* by Simon Vouet. *M* Les Halles

St-Germaine-l'Auxerrois, 1st. 13c-18c church of the Louvre Palace, mausoleum of royal artists and architects, a fine 15c porch. Royal pew is a tour-de-force in carved wood by Le Brun and Mercier. *M* Pont-Neuf

St-Gervais-St-Protais, 4th. Begun in the 15c, the handsome classical façade is 1616-21. The burial place of several artists and writers, and François Couperin was organist here. There are seven windows of painted glass (early 16c). *M* St-Paul

St-Merri, 4th. Rebuilt c 1520-2, with later additions, it claims the oldest bell in Paris (14c). Baroque pulpit and reliefs by M.A. and P.A. Slodtz, and chapel by Boffrand. Saint-Saëns was organist here. *M* Hôtel de Ville, Châtelet

St-Paul-St-Louis, 4th. Jesuit church built 1627-41 with a handsome Baroque portal and large dome. *Christ in the Garden* by Delacroix, and *Louis XIII offering a Model of the Church to St Louis* by Simon Vouet. *M* St-Paul

Tour St Jacques, 1st. A late Gothic tower (1508-22) (under restoration), is all that remains of a church on the old pilgrimage route. *M* Châtelet

commercial galleries

Alain Blondel, 4 rue Aubry-le-Boucher, 4th; Mon-Fri 11.00-13.00, 14.00-19.00, Sat 14.00-19.00; *T* 01 42 78 66 67, www.galerie-blondel.com. In the Beaubourg, a gallery showing contemporary figurative works. *M* Rambuteau

Chourlet, 2 & 4 pl des Vosges, 4th, *T* 01 42 76 04 09, www.chourlet.com, Strong floral works by painter Céline Chourlet, and animal sculptures. *M* Bastille

Eric Dupon, 13 rue Chapon, 3rd, *T* 01 44 54 04 14, www.od-arts.com/dupont. *M* Arts-et-Métiers

Filles-du-Jour Agnès B, 44 rue Quincampoix, 4th, *T* 01 44 54 55 90, www.galeriedujour.com. Enthusiastic art patron and famous designer, Agnès B is also a photographer and exhibits (about 10 times a year) work by artists and photographers. Reach the gallery via her library. *M* Rambuteau

La Galerie CSAO, 15 rue Elzévir, 3rd; open 12.00-19.00; *T* 01 44 54 90 50.
Traditional and contemporary Senegalese and West African art.
M St-Paul

G-Module, 15 rue Debelleyme, 3rd; Wed-Sat 12.00-19.00; *T* 01 42 71 14 75,
www.g-module. com. The window on young American artists who work
in New York: embracing all media. *M* Filles du Calvaire

Thessa Herold, 7 rue de Thorigny, 3rd; Tues-Fri 14.00-18.30, Sat 11.00-
18.30; *T* 01 42 78 78 68. Established in 1970, important gallery
showcasing a range of contemporary works.
M Sébastien-Froissart, Calvaire

Naïfs du Monde Entier, 8 rue du Pas-de-la-Mule, 3rd, *T* 01 42 78 71 57,
www.artnaif.net. Naive art from all over the world. *M* St-Paul, Bastille

Paris Musées, 29bis rue des Francs-Bourgeois, 4th; Tues-Fri 11.00-
13.00, 14.00-19.00, Mon and Sat 14.00-19.00, Sun 12.00-19.30;
T 01 42 74 13 02. Sales outlet for objects inspired by works, permanent
and temporary, in museums of the Ville de Paris.
M St-Paul, Chemin Vert

St-Merri, 9 rue St-Merri, 4th, *T* 01 42 77 39 12, www.artinuitparis.com.
Specialist in Inuit art made by the people of northern Canada, old and
contemporary. *M* Hôtel-de-Ville

eating and drinking

The Beaubourg and especially
the Marais are great places for
eating out. There is a huge
variety of French and ethnic
food, whether you're looking for
trendy expensive or smart
good-value. There are cafés
with terraces around the
Pompidou Centre and on the
elegant place des Vosges. Less

Le Georges, Centre Pompidou

obvious is place Ste-Catherine which has a number of attractive restaurants, and informal brasseries can be found on place Bourg-Tibourg. These *quartiers* are not lacking in bars, mostly laid-back and not particularly sophisticated, where the young crowd gather.

AT THE MUSEUMS

CENTRE POMPIDOU
Open to non-ticket holders, disabled access.

€   **Café** on the mezzanine of the entrance hall.

€€ **Le Georges**, 6th floor, *T* 01 44 78 47 99, 12.00-2.00, closed Tues. Smart Frères Costes establishment embellished with huge amorphous aluminium shapes. Superb panoramas of Paris; good-weather terrace. Dishes sound fancy but don't always match description.

MUSÉE D'ART ET D'HISTOIRE DU JUDAÏSME
€   **Café** open to non-ticket holders.

SURROUNDING AREA

€   **L'As du Fallafel**, 34 rue des Rosiers, 4th, *T* 01 48 87 63 60; closed Sat. Quite the best falafels, to take away or eat inside. *M* St-Paul

Barbara Bui Café, 27 rue Etienne-Marcel, 1st, *T* 01 45 08 04 04. Minimalist décor in this designer café which is a favourite place among fashionable trendies for a light lunch during shopping expeditions. *M* Etienne-Marcel

Comptoir Paris-Marrakech, 37 rue Berger, 1st, *T* 01 40 26 26 66. A trendy place where Middle-Eastern and Indian cooking blend in surroundings merging Paris and the Orient. *M* Louvre-Rivoli, Les Halles

Entre Ciel et Terre, 5 rue Hérold, 1st, *T* 01 45 08 49 84. Healthy eating near the stock exchange, mainly (not totally) vegetarian fare in smoke-free ambience. Paintings on show. *M* Les Halles, Louvre-Rivoli

Mariage Frères, 30-32 rue du Bourg-Tibourg, 4th, *T* 01 42 72 28 11; daily 12.00-19.00. Fashionable, almost snooty, tea room and shop, good for brunch, light lunch or luscious French pastry. (Also 13 rue des Grands-Augustins, 6th.) *M* Hôtel-de-Ville

Chez Marianne, 2 rue des Hospitalières-St-Gervais, 4th, *T* 01 42 72

18 86. Always packed and no wonder because the delicious Middle Eastern mezes and sweets are tempting and inexpensive; also takeaway. *M* St-Paul

Chez Max, 47 rue St-Honoré, 1st, *T* 01 45 08 80 13. A first floor dive with unsubtle décor, the place to go when strapped for cash. The good-value set menus include a drop of plonk. *M* Les Halles

Le Pain Quotidien, 18 rue des Archives, 4th, *T* 01 44 54 03 07; daily 7.00-19.00. Belgian chain offering salads, sandwiches and brunch. Good shoppers' stop. *M* Rambuteau

Pain Vin Fromage, 3 rue Geoffrey l'Angevin, 4th, *T* 01 42 74 07 52. Tucked away behind the Pompidou, you will find all kinds of cheesy delights - a choice of some 60 types; also hot dishes including fondues, racklettes, and salads. *M* Rambuteau

Le Petit Dakar, 6 rue Elzévir, 3rd, *T* 01 44 59 34 74. Senegalese cooking where fish features; also tasty chicken in grain sauce; reasonable prices. *M* St-Paul, Chemin Ver

404 Restaurant Familial, 69 rue des Gravilliers, 3rd, *T* 01 42 74 57 81. A private house transformed into a Moroccan restaurant - a very popular place but a little off the beaten track. *M* Arts et Métiers

Toupary, La Samaritaine, 2 quai du Louvre, 1st, *T* 01 40 41 29 29. Mediocre food but panoramic views from the terrace of the restaurant on the 5th floor of La Samaritaine department store. Lunch menus from €13.50 to €27.50. *M* Pont-Neuf

Les Vins des Pyrénées, 25 rue Beautreillis, 4th, *T* 01 42 72 64 94; closed Sun. A wine bar which proves that Paris has not had to go entirely techno-funk, either in décor or in food, to attract a young crowd. The prices are comforting. Great desserts. *M* St-Paul

€€ Anahï, 49 rue Volta, 3rd, *T* 01 48 87 88 24. Argentinian restaurant with an un-obvious entrance, popular with local fashion folk. *M* Arts et Métiers

Auberge de Jarente, 7 rue de Jarente, 4th, *T* 01 42 77 49 35. Specializing in hearty French Basque cooking, the ingredients include plenty of fish, hot peppers and, of course, *gâteau Basque*. Good value set menus. *M* St-Paul

Baracane, 38 rue des Tournelles, 4th, *T* 01 42 71 43 33; closed Sat midday, Sun. Sample the excellent ingredients and cooking of southwest France such as *foie gras*, *magret de canard* and *cassoulet*, at reasonable prices. *M* Bastille, Chemin-Vert

Benoît, 20 rue St-Martin, 4th, *T* 01 42 72 25 76. Confident and established, this family-run bistrot is on the expensive side but the food (excellent charcuterie, *blanquette de veau*, *boeuf mode* and *soufflé au grand marnier*) and ambience are worth paying for. *M* Hôtel de Ville

Au Bistrot de la Place, 2 pl du Marché Ste-Catherine, 4th, *T* 01 42 78 31 32; closed Sun. The greatest charm of this restaurant is its position in an attractive square near place des Vosges. *M* St-Paul, Bastille

Bofinger, 5-7 rue de la Bastille, 4th, *T* 01 42 72 87 82; open until 1.00. Classic brasserie in the Flo chain with marvellous glass dome, where you should be assured of a good meal although quality and service can slip. *M* Bastille

Ma Bourgogne, 19 pl des Vosges, 4th, *T* 01 42 78 44 64. A bit of a tourist trap, but fun to sit under the arcades of the Place des Vosges - inside is less obvious. The food is unsophisticated but standard. *M* St-Paul, Bastille

Le Dôme du Marais, 53bis rue des Francs-Bourgeois, 4th, *T* 01 42 74 54 17; closed Sat-Sun. Tucked away in a courtyard, this is an extraordinary building with a cupola over the dining area. The food is generally good with reasonably-priced set menus. *M* Rambuteau

Le Dos de la Baleine, 40 rue des Blancs-Manteaux, 4th, *T* 01 42 72 38 98; closed Mon, Sat, Sun midday. Relatively expensive for what you get, but an attractive place which draws an in-crowd and offers an interesting slant on the usual French dishes. *M* Hôtel-de-Ville, Rambuteau

L'Excuse, 14 rue Charles, 4th, *T* 01 42 77 98 97; closed Sun-Mon. A charming and intimate restaurant, slightly pricey, but lunch menu under €25 and dinner around €30. The food is consistently good and varies according to the season. *M* St-Paul

Le Grizzli, 7 rue St-Martin, 4th, *T* 01 48 87 77 56; closed Sun. Handy for the Pompidou Centre, with pavement terrace for sunny days and atmospheric interior at other times. The food is nicely varied, with interesting salads and desserts. *M* Hôtel de Ville

Chez La Vieille, **Adrienne**, 1 rue Bailleul/37 rue de l'Abre-Sec, 1st, *T* 01 42 61 68 04; Mon-Fri. Good, old-fashioned bistrot serving hearty portions. *M* Louvre-Rivoli

Au Pied de Cochon, 6 rue Coquillière, 1st, *T* 01 40 13 77 00. Although it has been here for ever, this popular 24-hour brasserie maintains a high standard in onion soup and pigs' trotters and other traditional dishes. Fairly pricey. *M* Les Halles

Saudade, 34 rue des Bourdonnais, 1st, *T* 01 42 36 03 65. A charming Portuguese restaurant which is well respected. The predominance of fish dishes includes several using salt cod; also non-fish Portuguese specialities. *M* Châtelet

La Tour de Montlhéry (Chez Denise), 5 rue des Prouvaires, 1st, *T* 01 42 36 21 82; open Mon-Fri, 24 hours a day, until 7.00 on Sat. Bustling, cheery, well-established Les Halles bistrot which continues to serve traditional, hearty, meaty dishes such as snails or steak. *M* Les Halles

€€€ L'Ambroisie, 9 pl des Vosges, 4th, *T* 01 42 78 51 45. For a major blow-out and damn the expense, this is a famous and wonderful place set in a 17c mansion with a high ratio of lackeys to customers, and excellent food. *M* Bastille, St-Paul

L'Osteria, 10 rue de Sévigné, 4th, *T* 01 42 71 37 08. An Italian restaurant whose reputation for risotto is unequalled. No signs or menu to advertise it, and simplicity inside, but the cooking is marvellous. *M* St-Paul

BARS

Bar de l'Entre'acte, 47 rue Montpensier, 1st, *T* 01 42 97 57 76. Theatrical and chaotic bar to the west of Palais Royal gardens, always hugely popular. *M* Louvre-Palais-Royal

La Belle Hortense, 31 rue Vieille du Temple, 4th, *T* 01 48 04 71 60; until 2.00am. A 'cool' bookshop where you can drink or chat until the early hours. *M* St-Paul

La Bodeguita del Medio, 10 rue des Lombards, 1st, *T* 01 44 59 66 90; Tues-Sat, until 1.30. Bar with authentic Cuban group and dancing. Free weekdays. *M* Châtelet

Caves Saint-Gilles, 4 rue Saint-Gilles, 3rd, *T* 01 48 87 22 62. A friendly Franco-Spanish tapas bar; huge paella dished up on Sundays. *M* Chemin-Vert

Le Comptoir, 37 rue Berger, 1st, *T* 01 40 26 26 66. Sink into Moroccan-style comfort and colour with an exotic cocktail or a soothing mint tea. *M* Châtelet

L'Enoteca, 25 rue Charles-V, 4th, *T* 01 42 78 91 44. Choose the ground-floor setting to relax and sample the 300 Italian wines on offer, accompanied by delicious Italian cooking at moderate prices. *M* St-Paul, Bastille

Les Etages, 35 rue Vieille-du-Temple, 4th, *T* 01 42 78 72 00; daily until 2.00. Charming Belle Epoque interior for this bar with cocktails from €4. *M* St-Paul

Jokko, 5 rue Elzévir, 3rd, *T* 01 42 74 35 96. Bar-Expos, Senegalese and West African contemporary works. *M* St-Paul, Chemin Vert

Juveniles, 47 rue de Richelieu, 1st, *T* 01 42 97 46 49. An extremely popular place (an offshoot of the British run Willi's Wine Bar) serving wine and spirits, tapas and light meals. *M* Palais-Royal

Pari's Aller Retour, 25 rue de Turenne, 4th, *T* 01 40 27 03 82. Concert-bar with music every evening at 20.30 (Sun 19.00). French songs and experimental film, paintings and photos. €9. *M* St-Paul

Au Petit Fer à Cheval, 30 rue Vieille-du-Temple, 4th, *T* 01 42 72 47 47; open 9.00 to 2.00. A small bar with plenty of atmosphere, and patronized largely by locals. A simple menu is on offer with daily specials. *M* Hôtel-de-Ville, St-Paul

Le Rouge Gorge, 8 rue St-Paul, 4th, *T* 01 48 04 75 89. There is a good selection to choose from at this wine bar in an old building. *M* St-Paul

Wine and Bubbles, 3 rue Française, 1st, *T* 01 44 78 99 84; open until 2.00, closed Sun. A small wine and champagne terrace. *M* Les Halles, Etienne Marcel

shopping

Both the Beaubourg and the Marais have fun and varied places to shop and are slightly less expensive than the 6/7th or 8th *arrondissements*, despite a good spattering of designer names. The Forum des Halles, 1-7 rue Pierre Lescot, 1st, is a four-level below-ground shopping precinct in the Beaubourg with some 50 designer boutiques. Access is on place des Halles (*M* Chatelet). There is a colourful flower market on the Ile de la Cité (see Flowers), and at the same place and same time on Sunday is a bird market (*M* Cité), while small animals and birds are sold on quai de la Mégisserie (*M* Pont-Neuf/Châtelet) every day 10.00-19.00. Very special to Paris are the *bouquinistes* (see Books). The Marais has become a hugely popular area for the young, arty, gays, and smart eccentrics or 'bobos' (bohemian-bourgeois) and is one of the few *quartiers* where you can shop on a Sunday. To experience everything from kosher delis to funky designer originals, head for rue des Francs Bourgeois and rue des Rosiers, whereas rue de Turenne is the place to find men's clothing at wholesale prices - anything from suits to accessories.

ACCESSORIES

Antik Batik, 18 rue de Turenne, 4th, *T* 01 44 78 02 00. French designs created from Indian batiks - clothes for men, women and children. *M* St-Paul

CSAO Boutique, 3 rue Elzévir, 3rd, *T* 01 44 54 55 88. Colourful hand woven and dyed cloth, furniture, wickerwork, objects from recycling, made in Senegal and West Africa. (See also Commercial Galleries.) *M* St-Paul, Chemin Vert

Des Pieds et des Mains, 22 passage Molière, 3rd, *T* 01 42 77 53 50; Fri-Sat 14.00-18.00 or by appointment. A novel, personalized souvenir - have a plaster cast made of a loved-one's hands and feet. *M* Rambuteau

DOM, 21 rue Ste-Croix-la-Bretonnerie, 4th, *T* 01 42 71 08 00. 70s inspired German-made objects, large and small, which are fun although bordering on kitsch. Good for presents. *M* Hôtel de Ville, St-Paul

Losco, rue de Sévigné, 4th, *T* 01 48 04 39 93; Tues 14.00-19.00, Wed-Sat 11.00-19.00. Hand-made belts. *M* St-Paul/Chemin Vert

Victor Chance, 17 rue Pavée, 4th, *T* 01 42 71 18 00; Tues-Sat, Sun and Mon afternoons. French designed handbags and travel accessories, both practical and original. *M* St-Paul

BOOKS

Bouquinistes, quai du Louvre to quai de l'Hotel de Ville, 1st and 4th. Along the quays, this is a traditional, semi-permanent open-air

Bouquinistes

market dealing in second-hand - sometimes rare - books and engravings. The goods are picturesquely crammed into green lock-up boxes attached to the walls bordering the sidewalks. (See also Left Bank.) *M* Pont-Neuf, Hôtel de Ville

LEKS, 19 rue Pierre Lescot, 1st, *T* 01 40 26 21 83. Specialist in books on the graphic arts, design and photography, mainly in English. *M* Etienne Marcel

CLOTHES

Azzedine Alaia, 7 rue de Moussy, 4th, *T* 01 42 72 19 19. Off-the-peg designs for women by this Tunisian-born designer. Discounted collections at 81 rue de la Verrerie. *M* St-Paul

Barbara Bui, 23 rue Etienne Marcel, 2nd, *T* 01 40 26 43 65. Funky clothes for the city dweller; café at no. 27. *M* Etienne Marcel

Bel Air, 2 rue des Rosiers, 4th, *T* 01 48 04 82 16; Mon-Sat, also Sun 14.00-19.30. Young, sexy clothes at reasonable prices. *M* St-Paul

Claude Zana, 115 rue de Turbigo, 2nd, *T* 01 44 88 29 96; Tues-Sat 11.00-19.00. Relaxed and elegant designs at affordable prices. *M* Arts et Metiers

Des Filles à la Vanille, 54 rue Tiquetonne, 2nd, *T* 01 42 36 47 77; open until 20.00. Fun, trendy and inexpensive clothes. *M* Etienne-Marcel

L'Eclaireur, 3ter rue des Rosiers, 4th (see also St-Germain, 6th), *T* 01 48 87 10 22. This is one of the most trendy and popular shops in Paris, selling accessories and clothes by all top designers. *M* St-Paul

Issey Miyake, 3 pl des Vosges, 4th, *T* 01 48 87 01 86. Revolutionary Japanese designer of novel and beautiful but expensive, fashions for men and women. Also **Pleats Please**, 3bis rue des Rosiers, 4th, *T* 01 43 14 78 78. This is Miyake's colourful innovative second line featuring permanent pleats. And **A-POC**, 'cut-it-yourself' collection, at 47 rue des Francs Bourgeois, 4th. *M* St-Paul

Kabuki, 25 rue Etienne Marcel, 1st, *T* 01 42 33 55 65. Designer clothes and shoes by well-known names. *M* Etienne-Marcel

Made in Sport, 33 rue Quincampoix, 4th, *T* 01 44 61 80 41. Famous sportswear, more for the look than for the sport. *M* Rambuteau

Spontini, 29 rue des Francs Bourgeois, 4th, *T* 01 44 78 80 71. Italian clothes for men - from casual to elegant - filling an important gap in men's wear. *M* St-Paul

Surface 2 Air, 49 rue de l'Arbre-Sec, 1st, *T* 01 49 27 04 54. A funky concept store which sells a whole range of items, including sought-after designer clothes and CDs, art, etc. *M* Châtelet-Les-Halles

Tsumori Chisato, 20 rue Barbette, 3rd, *T* 01 42 78 18 88. Slightly ironic but colourful clothes in lovely fabrics by this Japanese designer. *M* St-Paul

Yohji Yamamoto, 47 rue Etienne Marcel, 1st, *T* 01 45 08 82 45. Imaginative, flattering clothes for women by this leading Japanese designer. Designs for men, too. (Also rue de Grenelle and **Y's**, rue des Sts-Pères, 6th; rue du Louvre, 1st.) *M* Etienne-Marcel

Zadig et Voltaire, 36 rue de Sévigné, 4th, *T* 01 43 29 18 29. Elegant, sophisticated and up-to-date all-day wear. *M* St-Paul

DEPARTMENT STORES

La Samaritaine, 19 rue de la Monnaie, 1st, *T* 01 40 41 20 20. This long-established store has new owners and a new look. Vast range of brand-name fashions for men, women and children, as well as sports gear and home decorating. (See also Eating and Drinking.) *M* Pont-Neuf

FLOWERS

Au Nom de la Rose Diffusion, 87 rue St-Antoine, 4th, *T* 01 42 71 34 24. Roses and yet more romantic roses. (See also St-Germain, 6th.) *M* St-Paul, Bastille

Hysope & Cie, 104 rue Vieille du Temple, 3rd, *T* 01 44 59 33 00; daily 10.00-20.00. Flowers, vases and candles. *M* St-Paul

Marché aux fleurs, pl Louis Lépine, Ile de la Cité, 4th; daily 10.30-19.00. Wallow in the fragrance of the colourful flower market on the island. *M* Cité

La Rose du Désert, 27 rue des Rosiers, 4th, *T* 01 44 54 99 18; daily 10.00-23.00, closed Fri eve to Sat pm. Dry flowers as well as tea and cosmetics. *M* St-Paul

FOOD & WINE

Cacao et Chocolat, 36 rue Vieille du Temple, 4th, **T** 01 42 71 50 06. All types of chocolate; *dégustations* (tastings) offered. (Also at rue de Buci, 6th, and rue St-Louis-en-l'Isle, 4th.) **M** Hôtel de Ville

Drahonnet, 32 rue Vieille-du-Temple, 4th, **T** 01 42 72 78 01; Fri-Wed 7.00-21.30. Excellent boulangerie/patisserie. **M** St-Paul

La Ferme St-Aubin, 76 rue St-Louis-en-l'Ile, 4th, **T** 01 43 54 74 54; Tues-Sun 8.00-20.00, Sun 8.00-15.00. Sheer heaven for the cheese lover. **M** Pont-Marie, Sully-Morland

Florence Finkelsztajn, 24 rue des Ecouffes, 4th, **T** 01 48 87 92 85; Thur-Mon 10.00-19.00, and **Sacha Finkelsztajn**, 27 rue des Rosiers, 4th, **T** 01 42 72 78 91; Wed-Sun 10.00-19.00. You are spoilt for choice from the appetizing array of Jewish delicacies. **M** St-Paul

Izraël, 30 rue François-Miron, 4th, **T** 01 42 72 66 23. Claimed to represent the *monde des epices* (world of spices), this is a veritable Ali Baba's cave of world-wide food. **M** Hôtel-de-Ville

Au Levain du Marais, 32 rue de Turenne, 4th, **T** 01 42 78 07 31; Mon-Sat 7.00-20.00. Attractive red shop-front, and great variety of breads and pastries. **M** St-Paul

Mariage Frères, 30 rue du Bourg-Tibourg, 4th, **T** 01 42 72 28 11. Vast array of teas and everything to do with tea imbibing (see also restaurants). **M** Hôtel de Ville

HOMES

Anthéor, 11 rue Sévigné, 4th, **T** 01 40 27 91 25; daily 11.00-19.00, Sun 14.00-19.00. Pretty things for tables, well-designed and rainbow hued. **M** St-Paul

L'Art du Bureau, 47 rue des Francs Bourgeois, 4th, **T** 01 48 87 57 97; daily 10.30-19.00, Sun 14.00-19.00. Smart office accessories. **M** St-Paul.

Bô, 8 rue St-Merri, 4th, **T** 01 42 72 84 64; daily 11.00-19.30, Sun 14.00-19.30. Boutique-gallery with interesting and affordable contemporary household designs. **M** Rambuteau, Hôtel de Ville

Caravane, 6 rue Pavée, 4th, **T** 01 44 61 04 20. Sophisticated ethnic and exotic objects with lots of ideas for gifts and home accessories, as well as furniture. **M** St-Paul

Dehillerin, 10 rue Coquillière, 1st, **T** 01 42 36 53 13, www.e-dehillerin.fr.

A really great shop with a selection of kitchenware to send cooks delirious. **M** Les Halles

Litchi, 4 rue de Ecouffes, 4th, **T** 01 44 59 39 09, www.litchi.net. Bizarre *boutique-tendance* which celebrates the kitsch in everything, including - or especially - religious objects. Also paintings, lamps, jewellery, bags and Tarot reading on Friday afternoons. **M** St-Paul

Papier +, 9 rue du Pont Louis-Philippe, 4th, **T** 01 42 77 70 49. Multi-coloured paper, pencils and other stationery. **M** Pont-Marie

Salih Mekhici Design, 104 rue Vieille du Temple, 3rd, **T** 01 48 04 53 37. Lights and other decorative objects. **M** St-Paul

A. Simon, 48-52 rue Montmartre, 2nd, **T** 01 42 33 71 65. A vast range of professional cooking utensils of every shape and size. **M** Les Halles

Van der Straeten, 11 rue Ferdinand Duval, 4th, **T** 01 42 78 99 99. High-quality designer furniture made to order and fantasy jewellery. **M** St-Paul

JEWELLERY

Métal Pointu's, 19 rue des Francs-Bourgeois, 4th, **T** 01 40 29 44 34. Ethnically-modern styles in bronze, copper or solid silver which appeal to all ages. **M** St-Paul, Bastille

Gallery Aurus, 88 rue Quincampoix, 3rd, **T** 01 42 74 62 42. Fine modern jewellery. **M** Rambuteau

Harraca, 30 rue de Sévigné, 4th, **T** 01 40 27 02 71. (Also 89 rue St-Merry, 4th, **T** 01 42 78 21 19, and 9 rue des Canettes, 6th.) French designer who sculpts unusual and very modern jewellery in acrylic resin, gold and silver. **M** St-Paul

KIDS

Les Petits Bourgeois, 37 rue de Turenne, 3rd, **T** 01 48 04 38 38; Tues-Sat 11.00-19.00, Sun 14.00-19.00. A range of different trendy brands of clothes and shoes for children. **M** St-Paul

Unishop, 42 rue de Rivoli, 4th, **T** 01 42 72 62 84. End-of-range fashions for kids. **M** Hôtel-de-Ville

LINGERIE

Nulle Part Ailleurs, 15 rue Turbigo, 2nd, **T** 01 40 28 00 07. Around for some 20 years, but innovative and pioneering in the use of fabrics,

with lovely underwear and other garments in microfibre.
M Les Halles

MUSIC

Disc'King Rambuteau, 42 rue Quincampoix, 4th, *T* 01 42 36 03 45; daily
10.30-19.30, Sun 9.30-18.30. *M* Rambuteau

Extended, 42 rue Quincampoix, 4th, *T* 01 44 61 05 05; Tues-Sat. All types
of music, CD, DVD and LDV - new and second-hand.
M Châtelet, Les Halles

SHOES

Christian Louboutin, 19 rue J.-J.-Rousseau, 1st, *T* 01 42 36 05 31.
Strikingly novel footwear. *M* Les Halles (also St-Germain)

Kabuki, 25 rue Etienne-Marcel, 1st, *T* 01 42 33 55 65. Selection from top
designers; also clothes. *M* Etienne-Marcel

Michel Perry, 4 rue des Petits-Pères, 2nd, *T* 01 42 44 10 07. Intimate
boutique for men and women. *M* Pyramides

Un Dimanche à Venise, 7 rue des Francs Bourgeois, 4th, *T* 01 47 23 04 43
(see also 1st and 6th.) This boutique specializes in elegant Italian
shoes. *M* St-Paul

LEFT BANK
ST-MICHEL

Musée du Moyen Age

OPEN	9.15-17.45
CLOSED	Tues and PH
CHARGES	€5.50; under 25-year-olds and on Sun, €4. Admission free for under 18s, recipients of certain social benefits (unemployed/disabled); teachers. Valid proof of eligibility required for free admission and reductions. Admission free to all on the first Sunday of each month
TELEPHONE	01 53 73 78 00; information 01 53 73 78 16 (bookshop); 01 53 73 78 22
WWW.	musee-moyage.fr (for younger visitors)
MAIN ENTRANCE	6 pl Paul-Painlevé, 5th
METRO	Cluny-La Sorbonne, Odéon, St-Michel, RER St-Michel-Notre Dame
DISABLED ACCESS	01 53 73 78 04, 01 46 34 51 75 (fax). Sound and touch equipment for the visually impaired visitor
GUIDED VISIT	In English at 11.30 on Saturday
PUBLICATIONS	Orientation guide in English
PHOTOGRAPHY	Hand-held cameras are permitted but no flash or tripods
SHOP	Bookshop/boutique, 9.15-18.00 (open to non-ticket holders), has a large selection of books, CDs, cassettes, videos, CD-roms and gifts, related to the arts and music of the Middle Ages

The Musée du Moyen Age - Thermes et Hôtel de Cluny is an intimate museum of special charm housed in the 15c Hôtel de Cluny. The building is one of the finest extant examples of medieval French domestic architecture in Paris, flanked to the north by the best conserved vestige of antique Paris, the Gallo-Roman thermae. The superb collection of medieval arts and crafts in the museum ranges from gold artefacts of the Visigoth and Merovingian periods through remnants of stonecarving from Notre-Dame de Paris to tapestries. Since autumn 2000 it has been endowed with a medieval garden. The museum offers guided visits as well as lectures and cultural activities including concerts.

From the street, pass through an archway and in the right-hand corner of the courtyard you will see the entrance to the museum.

THE BUILDING

The property was bought in 1340 by Pierre de Chalus, Abbot of Cluny in Burgundy, to establish a residence in the area of the university. The present house, built by Abbot Jacques d'Amboise, dates from c 1490, but was rarely occupied by the abbots. It presents an early example of a house standing between a courtyard and a garden. Louis XII's widow, Mary Tudor (1496-1533), lived here for a while. At the Revolution the building

Hôtel de Cluny

became national property, and in 1833 was filled with the treasures collected by Alexandre du Sommerard (1771-1842). These were subsequently bought by the State and Alexandre's son Edmond became the first curator. The collection has been regularly supplemented by new acquisitions. The remains of the Roman baths became the repository of original stonework removed from major Parisian monuments during renovation.

HIGHLIGHTS

Medieval sculptures from Notre-Dame de Paris	Room 8
Gallo-Roman remains	Rooms 9, 12
6c Byzantine ivories	Room 10
15c tapestries, *The Lady with the Unicorn*	Room 13
7c Visigoth crowns; 14c *Golden Rose*	Room 16
11c Gold antipendium (altar front) from Basle	Room 19

GROUND FLOOR

ROOM 1 is the bookshop.

ROOMS 2-3 Exhibited here are some of the **tapestries** for which the museum is famous, including a set of six scenes illustrating the activities of a noble household of c 1500, entitled *La Vie Seigneuriale* c 1500-25. *The Resurrection* (c 1420) is the oldest tapestry in the museum. Part of the collection includes **textiles and embroidery** (6c-14c), of Coptic or Byzantine origin as well as French, Italian and Spanish. An example of the highly regarded English production of the early 14c is the *Embroidery with Leopards*, in gold on velvet, the stylized creatures surrounded by foliage and young girls.

Chess players (15c stained glass)

ROOM 6 Alabasters from Nottingham These small religious reliefs and sculptures were virtually mass-produced for the export market during the 14c and 15c. There is also a precious collection of recently-restored **stained glass** on display, including 12c fragments from Alsace, from Troyes and from St-Denis, Paris, and early to mid-13c pieces from the Sainte-Chapelle, Paris.

ROOMS 5 AND 7 Corridor linking the medieval and antique periods.

SALLE NOTRE-DAME-DE-PARIS *Room 8* A large space which is arranged for the exhibition of sculptural fragments removed from Notre-Dame de Paris during the Revolution. These include the original 13c heads from the gallery of the Kings of Judah, discovered in 1977 during excavation work in Rue de la Chaussée d'Antin; a magnificent *Adam*, c 1260; and a vigorous nude figure (heavily restored), which was originally painted, from the south transept.

ROOMS 10-11 Among the small carved ivories (4c-12c) is a sensual *Ariadne* from Constantinople (6c), and an English diptych (8c). The latter is remarkable because it is carved on both sides, having been reused in the 9c when it received decoration typical of the Carolingian Renaissance. Some fine **Romanesque capitals** from the abbey church of St-Germain-des-Prés (mid-11c) are on display, and two moving 12c French *Crucifixions* in polychrome wood from provincial France. Several Gothic statues originate from the Sainte-Chapelle, while fine carved stone retables from the Paris area include one from St-Denis of the *Baptism of Christ* (1250-60).

Ariadne (6c ivory)

ROOMS 9 AND 12 Below this room is the frigidarium of the **Gallo-Roman baths**, remarkable in that it still retains its 2c vault, unique in France. The room (20m by 11.5m and 14m in height), with the piscina on the northern side, is all that remains in its entirety of the baths, assumed to have been built during the 1c and modified later (212-217). Only parts of its tepidarium and caldarium, and the palestras (gymnasiums) facing blvd St-Germain remain, after demolition in the 16c and 19c. The museum's collection of Gallo-Roman sculpture is displayed here together with models of the baths and the Hôtel de Cluny.

FIRST FLOOR

ROOM 13 The major work in the museum is the series of six exquisite *millefleurs* **tapestries**, *La Dame à la Licorne* (The Lady and the Unicorn). These hangings are among the most famous in France, and are displayed in a specially designed circular, dimly lit room, with fibre optic lighting for conservation reasons. (There is also sound and touch equipment for the non-sighted, in French.)

The tapestries, probably designed by a Parisian artist but woven, in silk and wool, in the Netherlands between 1484 and 1500, were commissioned by Jean le Viste, a Lyonnais lawyer whose family

La Dame à La Licorne (1484-1500 tapestry)

arms are frequently repeated in the designs. The tapestries hung for a long time in the Château de Boussac in the Creuse until brought to public notice by both Prosper Mérimée, Inspector of Historic Monuments, and the writer George Sand. The works were acquired by the museum in 1882 and have been restored.

On rich red backgrounds with blue islands of colour and varied species of trees, the panels are scattered with thousands of delicate flower, animal and bird motifs. In each the Lady appears in different attire. She is sometimes accompanied by her maid and always flanked by the mythical, elusive unicorn, symbol of purity, as well as a lion. In several of the panels a monkey and a pet dog are also included.

Five of the tapestries present the theme of the Senses. *Taste*: the Lady feeds the monkey and a parakeet from a bowl of sweetmeats; *Hearing*, the Lady plays a portable organ; *Sight*, the unicorn gazes into the mirror held before him by the Lady; *Smell*, the monkey sniffs a flower while the Lady weaves a garland; and *Touch*, the Lady gently grasps the horn of the unicorn. Opposite and in isolation is the sixth tapestry in the series known by the enigmatic motto embroidered above the pavilion, *A mon seul désir* (To my only desire). The Lady is caught returning jewels to a casket which her maid is holding. The iconography of this panel remains a mystery.

LATE MEDIEVAL RELIGIOUS WORKS *Room 14* These come from all parts of Europe and include several altarpieces. One of the most noteworthy is the ***Altarpiece of the Blessed Sacrament*** (1513) from Averbode in Brabant the work of Jan de Molder, carved with the Mass of St Gregory in the centre and the Last Supper on the right. There are numerous representations of Virgins and female saints.

THE ARTS OF THE GOLDSMITHS AND ENAMELLERS *Room 16* The centrepieces of this glittering array are three **Visigothic votive crowns** with their pendant crosses, dating from the late 7c. The elegant *Golden Rose* (1330), was given by the Avignon Pope John XXII to a count of Neuchâtel and there is also Gallo-Roman and

Merovingian jewellery. Among examples of high-quality late 12c-14c Limoges enamelwork - chalices, pyxes, shrines, plaques, croziers, crucifixes - are two reliquaries of St Thomas Becket (1190-1200) with the scene of the Archbishop's assassination.

ROOM 18 contains choir-stalls with irreverently carved misericords (1492-1500), and illuminated manuscripts.

ROOM 19 The early-11c **gold antipendium** (altar front), part of the Basle treasure, which was possibly intended as a donation for Monte Cassino from Emperor Henry II and Empress Cunegonde, who are portrayed as miniscule figures at the feet of Christ.

ROOM 20 The **chapel** is Flamboyantly vaulted from a central pillar. It contains a series of 23 **tapestries** (continues in Room 19) depicting the *Life of St Stephen*, which was commissioned c 1500 by Jean Baillet, Bishop of Auxerre for the cathedral. They are in remarkable condition although never restored, with still strong colours and every painstaking detail clearly evident. The scenes are arranged in alternate interior and exterior settings, the first part dealing with the life and martyrdom of St Stephen and the second with the legend of the relics.

ROOMS 21-23 Italian works and small domestic artefacts such as late-medieval wooden combs, embroidered alms purses, tapestries, paintings, and arms and armour.

MEDIEVAL GARDENS

The garden (enter from blvd St-Germain) is a contemporary interpretation of themes and symbolism found in the museum. It is divided into distinct enclosed areas described, for example, as the *Forêt de la Licorne*, the *hortus conclusus*, the *Jardin céleste*, and the *Jardin d'amour* and there is also a terraced garden with medicinal and culinary plants.

on route

Ile de la Cité, 1st/4th, *M* Cité, is the geographic centre of Paris and the site of the original Gallic settlement of Lutèce or *Lutetia Parisiorum*, settled c 52 BC by the Romans. The long and important history of the Cité is reflected in its prestigious monuments:

Cathédrale de Notre-Dame, *T* 01 42 34 56 10. The cathedral of Paris, at the heart of the Cité, is a magnificent Gothic masterpiece (12c-13c). Emblematic of medieval Paris, the elegant west façade, which emerged glowingly bright after a Millennium restoration, is highlighted by its two **towers**; Mon-Fri 8.00-18.45, Sun 8.00-19.45; *T* 01 44 32 16 72. Climb 387 steps for views across the cathedral spires and down to the Seine, and past the great bell Emmanuel.

Cathédrale de Notre-Dame rose window

Crypte Archaéologique, 10.00-18.00, closed Mon and PH; *T* 01 43 29 83 51. The Gallo-Roman foundations beneath the cathedral forecourt.

Musée Notre-Dame, daily 14.30-18.00; *T* 01 43 25 42 92. History of the cathedral.

Mémorial aux Martyrs de la Déportation, sq Jean XXIII. Erected in 1962 in memory of French citizens deported to concentration camps during the Second World War.

Palais de la Cité-Conciergerie, 1 quai de l'Horloge, 1st; daily, April-Sept 9.30-18.30, Oct-March 10.00-17.00, closed 1/1, 1/5, 1/11, 11/11, 25/12; *T* 01 53 73 78 50. Medieval royal palace transformed into a prison in the 15c where Marie-Antoinette was incarcerated at the Revolution.

Sainte-Chapelle, 4 blvd du Palais, 1st, Hours as for Palais-Conciergerie above; *T* 01 53 73 78 50. Famous for its spectacular stained glass and Gothic architecture, the royal chapel on two levels was built in the mid-

13c by Louis IX to house the relic of the Crown of Thorns. **M** St-Michel-Notre-Dame

Arènes de Lutèce, rue des Arènes, 5th. 9.00-21.30; winter 8.00-17.30. The few remains of the 1c Gallo-Roman amphitheatre, now used for picnics or games of *boules*. **M** Jussieu

Eglise St-Etienne-du-Mont, pl du Panthéon, 5th; daily 9.00-19.30; closed 12.00-14.00 on Mon and Sat, Sun in July-Aug; **T** 01 43 54 11 79. Elegant 15c-16c church with the only existing rood screen in Paris and the tomb of Sainte Geneviève. **M** Cardinal-Lemoine

Eglise St-Séverin, 1 rue des Prêtres St-Séverin, 5th. Begun in the 12c, with notable doorway and ambulatory vaulting as well as modern glass. **M** Cluny-Sorbonne

Institut du Monde Arabe,1 rue des Fossés-St-Jacques, 5th; 10.00-18.00, closed Mon; **T** 01 40 51 38 38. Impressive building (1987) by Jean Nouvel with **museum** dedicated to Arabic and Islamic art and civilization, with objets d'art, calligraphy, etc. Also excellent temporary exhibitions, restaurants and boutique. **M** Jussieu

Ile St-Louis A delightful island with beautiful 17c façades where time has stood still. It seems fragilely attached to the mainland by its bridges. Despite the restaurants and visitors, it maintains an aura of calm. The small Baroque church of **St-Louis-en-l'Ile** is worth a visit.

Jardin du Luxembourg, 6th, gardens of 23 ha around the Palais du Luxembourg (temporary exhibitions), with statues. **RER** Luxembourg

Jardin des Plantes, 57 rue Cuvier, 5th, **T** 01 40 79 30 00. A pleasant botanical and zoological garden covering 24ha. Originally royal, it was created in 1635 and planted with a wide range of wild and herbaceous plants. In 1793 it became the Museum of Natural History encompassing several museums and galleries (palaeontology, mineralogy), and greenhouses. The **Grande Galerie de l'Evolution**, 10.00-18.00, closed Tues, **T** 01 40 79 39 00, has impressive displays which lead you through the story of evolution, and evoke the relationship between man and nature. **M** Jussieu

Mosquée de Paris, rue Quatrefages, 5th; 9.00-12.00, 14.00-18.00 (guided visits). Inspired by the mosques of Fez, the religious buildings are traditionally grouped around a courtyard. **M** Monge

Musée de la Monnaie, 11 quai Conti, 6th; 11.00-17.30 (Sat-Sun 12.00-17.30), closed Mon; **T** 01 40 46 55 35. Situated in the old Mint (Hôtel de la Monnaie), the history of French currency from Roman Gaul to the Revolution. **M** Pont-Neuf

Panthéon, pl du Panthéon, 5th; daily, April-Sept 9.30-18.30; Oct-March 10.00-18.15; closed 1/1, 1/5, 11/11, 25/12; *T* 01 44 32 18 00. Monumental domed church by Soufflot (1764-90), transformed into a shrine to France's great men (and women) such as Victor Hugo, Voltaire, Zola, Jean Moulin, André Malraux. Also Foucault's famous pendulum and exhibition. *M* Cardinal-Lemoine, *RER* Luxembourg

Quai des Grands Augustins, built in 1313, is the oldest riverside embankment in Paris, and takes its name from a convent which was here from the 13c and is lined with 14c-16c houses.

commercial galleries

Arcima, 161 rue St-Jacques, 5th, *T* 01 46 33 00 11. Specializes in the work of artists from countries such as Armenia, Iraq, Haiti and North Africa, including Saadi el Kaabi, graphic designer Moustafa Boutadgine and the textured works of Emannuelle Timini-Blanc. *M* Cluny-La Sorbonne

Arnoux, 27 rue Guénégaud, 6th, *T* 01 46 33 04 66. One of many on this street, it specializes in abstract painting of the 1950s - artists such as Karen Appel, Maurice Estève, Serge Poliakoff, David Malking. Promotes a select few young painters and sculptors. *M* Odéon

Montenay, 41 rue Mazarine, 6th, *T* 01 56 81 00 53. Contemporary works by young national and international artists. *M* Odéon

Vert Galant, 52 quai des Orfèvres, 1st, *T* 01 44 07 20 74. *M* Pont-Neuf

Anton Weller, 5 rue des Ursulines, 5th, *T* 01 42 72 05 62. Beltrame, Geleynse and Rousseau. *M* Luxembourg

eating and drinking

AT THE MUSEUM

INSTITUT DU MONDE ARABE
All closed Monday.

€ **Le Moucharabieth**, self-service restaurant, 12.00-14.30.

Café Littéraire on the ground floor, *T* 01 40 51 34 69; open 11.00-19.00. Comfortable café and tea-room.

€€ **Ziryab**, *T* 01 53 10 10 20; closed Sat evening/Sun. At the top of this eye-catching building, the view of Notre-Dame is stunning but the mainly North African dishes can be disappointing. Tea (mint) is served from 15.00.

SURROUNDING AREA

€ **Au 29**, 29 rue Dauphine, 6th, *T* 01 46 33 75 92. Small first-floor Lebanese restaurant with authentic cooking. *M* Odéon, Pont-Neuf

Berthillon, 31 rue St-Louis-en-l'Ile, 4th, *T* 01 43 54 31 61; Wed-Sun 10.00-20.00. The best-known name in Parisian ice cream, and it all started here on the Ile St-Louis. Always worth waiting in line to sample some of the 70 flavours on offer; also served in many cafés and restaurants. *M* Pont-Marie

La Cafetière, 21 rue Mazaine, 6th, *T* 01 46 33 76 90. Friendly Franco-Italian set-up on two floors with coffee-pot décor. Standard dishes (pastas, carpaccio), reasonable prices; lunch menu €23. *M* Odéon

La Charlotte en l'Ile, 24 rue St-Louis-en-l'Ile, 4th, *T* 01 43 54 25 83; closed Mon-Wed. A tea-shop packed with whimsical decorations to entertain all comers, with various teas, the thickest of hot chocolate and wicked chocolate tarts. *M* Pont-Marie

Huître et Demi, 80 rue Mouffetard, 5th, *T* 01 43 37 98 21. This is a reasonably priced fish restaurant in popular rue Mouffetard. Lunch menu as low €11 (Mon-Fri), and evening €17 and €28. *M* Place-Monge

Isami, 4 quai d'Orléans, 4th, *T* 01 40 46 06 97; closed Sun eve/Mon. This small bar on the Ile-St-Louis looking out to the Seine is the place to eat excellent sushi. *M* Pont-Marie

La Maison des Trois Thés, 33 rue Gracieuse, 5th, **T** 01 43 36 93 84. Tea-making rituals and more than a 1000 flavours of tea to choose from. Not just a cuppa - more like a happening. **M** Place Monge

Mosquée de Paris, 39 rue Geoffroy-St-Hilaire, 5th, **T** 01 43 31 38 20; 9.00-24.00. For a taste of the Orient, try the tea-room/garden next to the mosque where students pore over their books. Bottomless pot of sweetened mint tea and a selection of honeyed sweetmeats. *Hammam* (women: 10.00-21.00, Mon, Wed, Thur, Sat; men: Tues, Sun). **M** Censier-Daubenton

Le Mouffetard, 116 rue Mouffetard, 5th, **T** 01 43 31 42 50; daily 7.15-22.30. Pretty basic café which has been around for years. Fun to visit on market days for a pastry, a snack or something more substantial. **M** Censier-Daubenton

Chez Pento, 9 rue Cujas, 5th, **T** 01 43 26 81 54. This simple bistrot is popular with good reason, because the food, of the traditional variety, is very good and very affordable. **M** Cluny-La Sorbonne

Les Quatre et Une Saveurs, 72 rue du Cardinal-Lemoine, 5th, **T** 01 43 26 88 80; closed Sun eve/Mon. A popular Japanese vegetarian restaurant, where no sugar, dairy produce or eggs are used (even in the desserts), but the menu does include fish. All organic produce. **M** Cardinal-Lemoine

Tao, 248 rue St-Jacques, 5th, **T** 01 43 26 75 92; closed Sun. Tiny, functional, but good, tasty Vietnamese cooking. Budget prices. **M** Luxembourg

€€ **Alcazar**, 62 rue Mazarine, 6th, **T** 01 53 10 19 99. The venture by Terence Conran was considered audacious 5 years ago by Parisians, but the ultra simple décor, pleasant service and good quality menu - includes fish and chips - attracts the in-crowd. **M** Odéon

Allard, 41 rue St-André-des-Arts, 6th, **T** 01 43 26 48 23. One of the most famous and long-established bistrots in Paris where the food is reliably good but doesn't come cheap. **M** St-Michel

l'AOC, 14 rue des Fossés-St-Bernard, 5th, **T** 01 43 54 22 52; closed Sun-Mon. This is a cosy and friendly bistrot with good, fragrant home cooking and prices which won't leave you broke. **M** Jussieu, Cardinal-Lemoine

L'Atlas, 12 blvd St-Germain, 5th, **T** 01 46 33 86 98; closed Mon. Modern Moroccan cooking combining French and Arab ideas gives the tajine a whole new meaning. **M** Mauberg-Mutualité

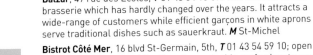

Balzar, 49 rue des Ecoles, *T* 01 43 54 13 67. This is a real 1930s' brasserie which has hardly changed over the years. It attracts a wide-range of customers while efficient garçons in white aprons serve traditional dishes such as sauerkraut. *M* St-Michel

Bistrot Côté Mer, 16 blvd St-Germain, 5th, *T* 01 43 54 59 10; open until 23.00. There is a friendly welcome to this seafood restaurant successfully run by top chef Michel Rostang's daughter. The quality of the fish is excellent and not over-priced, and there are some meat dishes on offer. Small terrace in front. *M* Maubert-Mutualité

Les Bookinistes, 53 quai des Grands-Augustins, 6th, *T* 01 43 25 45 94. An appealing address with a warm welcome, owned by master chef Guy Savoy. Specializes in fish dishes, beautifully presented. The disadvantage is the two sittings policy. *M* Odéon, St-Michel

Au Bouillon Racine, 3 rue Racine, 6th, *T* 01 44 32 15 60. Installed in this splendid restored Art Nouveau building is a Belgium brasserie on two floors - bar downstairs, smarter space upstairs. The cuisine is modern Flemish and the changing set menus are fairly easy on the wallet. *M* Cluny-La Sorbonne

Brasserie de l'Ile St-Louis, 55 quai de Bourbon, 4th, *T* 01 43 54 02 59; daily 12.00-1.00, except Thur 17.00-1.00. Hardly changed since the 1960s, its main asset is the view across the Seine to Notre-Dame from the terrace, a great place for a beer. Inside, beyond the bar, are long rustic tables where basic brasserie fare is served - just don't expect a gastronomic revelation. *M* Pont-Marie

Au Buisson Ardent, 25 rue Jussieu, *T* 01 43 54 93 02; closed Sat-Sun. Reliably good cooking using fresh ingredients, this modern-style bistrot is popular and the lunch menu is very good value. *M* Jussieu

Chez Clément, 9 pl St-André-des-Arts, 6th, *T* 01 56 81 32 00. A chain of some dozen restaurants decorated with old kitchen or garden tools, and patchwork. Specializes in fish dishes and roast meat. Menu €15. *M* St-Michel

L'Equitable, 1 des Fossés-St-Marcel, 5th, *T* 01 43 31 69 20; closed Sun eve and Mon. A little beyond the Jardin des Plantes, this restaurant which started out with great panache, serving imaginative dishes based on traditional ingredients, has lost a little of its edge. *M* St-Marcel, Les-Gobelins, Censier

L'Espadon Bleu, 25 rue des Grands-Augustins, 6th, *T* 01 46 33 00 85. Part of the Jacques Cagna empire, this is a small, brightly coloured, fish restaurant where standards are maintained. *M* St-Michel, Odéon

Fogon St-Julien, 10 rue St-Julien-le-Pauvre, 5th, *T* 01 43 54 31 33; open until 1.30, closed Sun. Excellent traditional Spanish cooking with several different types of paella, as well as tapas, savoury and sweet. Altogether a good eating experience in a very attractive setting. *M* St-Michel

Les Fontaines, 9 rue Soufflot, 5th, *T* 01 43 26 42 80; closed Sat eve and Sun. Never mind the décor, which is a total non-event, but concentrate on the hearty helpings of simple, good bistrot food and the warm welcome. Good value. *M* Cluny-La Sorbonne

Chez Maître Paul, 12 rue Monsieur-le-Prince, *T* 01 43 54 74 59. The cuisine of the Franche-Comté is well presented to a high standard with some excellent chicken dishes and asparagus when in season. *M* Odéon

Mavrommatis, 42 rue Daubenton, 5th, *T* 01 43 31 17 17; closed Mon. Bright and elegant, this is the best and most authentic Greek cooking around. The moussaka is superb and there is an excellent range of Greek wine. Lunch menu around €19.
M Censier-Daubenton

Au Moulin a Vent - Chez Henri, 20 rue des Fossés-St-Bernard, 5th, *T* 01 43 54 99 37; losed Sat midday and Sun. This bistrot is so incredibly authentic that it might be a pastiche. But it's the real thing and serves excellent beef, as well as snails, frogs' legs and *andouillettes* (sausages) in generous portions. *M* Jussieu, Cardinal-Lemoine

L'Orangerie, 28 rue St-Louis-en-l'Ile, 4th, *T* 01 46 33 93 98. A romantic setting for dinner only. The *carte-menu* for €65, including wine, features, for example, *haricots verts frais au foie gras d'oie*. *M* Pont-Marie

Le Procope, 13 rue de l'Ancienne Comédie, 6th, *T* 01 40 46 79 00. Established 1686 and considered something of a tourist trap, but the wonderful building on three floors has been renovated and has an attractive menu of adequate quality. *M* St-Michel, Odéon

Le Reminet, 3 rue des Grands-Degrés, 5th, *T* 01 44 07 04 24. Miniscule bistrot with stone walls, which tends to become very crowded. The innovative menu takes traditional dishes and gives them an unusual variation. The desserts are worth leaving space for. *M* Maubert-Mutualité

Chez Réné, 14 blvd St-Germain, 5th, *T* 01 43 54 30 23. This is a great example of a classic Parisian bistrot, and what's more it has conserved its 1950s décor. Service is down to earth, as is the cooking, which delivers timeless favourites such as *cochonnailles* (pork), *boeuf bourguignon* and profiteroles. *M* Maubert-Mutualité

La Rôtisserie d'en Face, 2 rue Christine, *T* 01 43 26 40 98. Good, simple food, spacious setting, lunchtime menus are reasonable. *M* St-Michel, Odéon

Le Vieux Bistro, 14 rue du Cloître-Notre-Dame, 4th, *T* 01 43 54 18 95. The exterior is unassuming, but the traditional and timeless French dishes such as *poireaux vinaigrettes* (leeks in vinaigrette), *cuisses de grenouille* (frogs' legs), *boeuf bourguignon*, *tarte Tatin*, are beautifully cooked. *M* Cité

€€€ **Lapérouse**, 51 quai des Grands-Augustins, 6th, *T* 01 43 26 68 04. An old favourite that's been here for ages and has had its ups and downs. But it's in good hands now, with a young chef who is doing a great job. Menus €30 (lunch), and €84. *M* St-Michel

La Tour d'Argent, 15-17 quai de la Tournelle, 5th, *T* 01 43 54 23 31; closed Mon and midday Tues. This is such an institution on the Left Bank that it has to be mentioned if way above most people's budget. But don't despair, the lunch menu is around €60 and worth every cent for the experience of that wonderful glass room with a view and, of course, the cuisine. The most celebrated of its dishes are the *quenelles de brochet* (pike dumplings) and *caneton Tour d'Argent* (duck). The wine list is formidable and the cellars can be visited. Also small **Musée de la Table**. *M* Pont-Marie, Cardinal-Lemoine

BARS

Le Bar Dix, 10 rue de l' Odéon, 6th, *T* 01 43 26 66 83. An old favourite with young locals and students, cheap sangria and jukebox accompaniment. *M* Odéon

Café Contrescarpe, 57 rue Lapécède, 5th, *T* 01 43 36 82 88; open every day, 21.00-3.00. Cosy, welcoming bar-restaurant with garden terrace in summer. *M* Place-Monge

Café Delmas, 2 place de la Contrescarpe, 5th, *T* 01 43 26 51 26; daily 7.30-2.00 and to 4.00 at weekends. Traditional French bar-restaurant on the square with view of the fountain. *M* Place-Monge

Le Café Egyptien, 112-114 rue Mouffetard (enter by rue de l'Arbalète), 5th, *T* 01 43 31 11 35. A taste of the Orient and sociable surroundings where you can have a gentle draw on a hubble-bubble. *M* Censier-Daubenton

Café Orbital, 13 rue de Médicis, 6th, *T* 01 43 25 76 77,
www.cafeorbital.com; open 9.00-22.00. This café-internet was
where Parisians first got connected. *M* Luxembourg

Café Oz, 184 rue St-Jacques, 5th, *T* 01 43 54 30 48. Oz-tralie bar,
with quasi Aborigine décor, a sort of bohemian Harry's Bar.
M Luxembourg

Le Comptoir du Relais, 5 carrefour de l' Odéon, 6th, *T* 01 43 29 12 05.
Essentially a wine bar, all tiles and mirrors. *M* Odéon

Les Etages St-Germain, 5 rue Buci, 6th, *T* 01 46 34 26 26; open until
2.00. Brightly coloured mosaics give this a feel of a Spanish tapas
bar. *M* Mabillon, St-Germain-des-Prés

La Méthode, 2 rue Descartes, 5th, *T* 01 43 54 22 43; open weekdays
until 4.00am, Fri-Sat to 5.00. Very friendly bar on a small square.
M Maubert-Mutualité

shopping

Unlike neighbouring St-Germain, the student quarter, St-Michel,
is not a mainstream shopping area. However, rue Monsieur-le-
Prince offers some interesting browsing, and bookshops and
music stores are legion. Rue
Mouffetard, leading off the
picturesque place de la
Contrescarpe in the heart of the
Quartier Latin, is always bustling
and active, even on a Sunday. One
of the favourite markets of central
Paris is held here (Tuesday-
Saturday all day, and Sunday
morning), and the smaller Carmes
market (Tuesday, Thursday,
Saturday) is on place Maubert.

Cheese display in Rue Mouffetard

ACCESSORIES

Bazaar ding dong, 24 rue Mouffetard, 5th, *T* 01 43 37 58 68. Second-hand accessories and clothes. *M* Place-Monge

Kazana, 47/49 rue Mouffetard, 5th, *T* 01 43 36 19 02. Shawls and jewellery in a vast range of colours. *M* Place-Monge

Le Pied, 105 rue Monge, 5th, *T* 01 55 43 86 61. Everything for the foot! Socks, stockings and so on. *M* Place-Monge

BOOKS

Bouquinistes Traditional market along the quays dealing in second-hand books (see also Beaubourg-Marais). *M* St-Michel

Librarie Gourmande, 4 rue Dante, 6th, *T* 01 43 54 37 27. Specializes in books for cooks and foodies. *M* St-Michel

La Librarie des Gourmets, 98 rue Monge, *T* 01 43 31 16 42. Mainly French, but a myriad of books on food and wine; how about a cook book exclusively on *Le crumble* for example? *M* Censier-Daubenton

Maxi-Livres, 16 blvd St-Michel, *T* 01 43 25 85 02, and 31 rue des Ecoles, 3rd, *T* 01 43 29 47 43. Cut-price bookshops. (Also St-André-des-Arts, 6th.) *M* St-Michel, Cluny-La Sorbonne

CLOTHES

Chromatic, 67 rue Mouffetard, 5th, *T* 01 45 87 08 93; open every day, 10.30-20.00. Different designers for casual fun clothes, no. 92 for more elegant ones. *M* Place-Monge

Filles à la Vanille, 79 rue Mouffetard, 5th, *T* 01 47 07 46 64. Little shop with lots of original styles at attractive prices. Open every day until 20.00. *M* Place-Monge

Kimono, 37 rue Monge, 5th, *T* 01 43 29 01 17. Modernized Asian designs of unusual styles in dresses and trousers. *M* Cardinal-Lemoine

Pierre Samary, 9 rue des Quatre-Vents, 6th, *T* 01 46 33 59 99. Elegant, stylish clothes for the laid-back man. *M* Odéon

René Derhy, 53 blvd St-Michel, 5th, *T* 01 43 54 14 41. French designer for feminine light clothes in light materials, flowery and colourful. *M* St-Michel

FLOWERS

A. Flory, 29 rue Monge, 5th, *T* 01 56 24 30 31. Little flower shop open every day from 9.00-21.00. *M* Cardinal-Lemoine

Monceau Fleurs, 104 rue Monge, 5th, *T* 01 47 07 17 94. French chain flower shop. A big range at reasonable prices. *M* Place-Monge, Censier-Daubenton

FOOD

Charcuterie Charles, 10 rue Dauphine, 6th, *T* 01 43 54 25 19. Traditional high-quality cooked meats, French sausages and other deli foods. *M* Odéon

Charcuterie Coesnon, 30 rue Dauphine, 6th, *T* 01 43 54 35 80; Tues-Sat 8.30-19.00. Hand-crafted pork-meat sausages of all types, *foie gras* and prepared dishes. *M* Odéon

Hediard, 118 rue Monge, 5th, *T* 01 43 31 88 94. Famous French delicatessen. *M* Censier-Daubenton

Kayser, 8 rue Monge, 5th, *T* 01 44 07 01 42. Just what you always hope for when buying bread or pastries in Paris. *M* Maubert-Mutualité

Mavrommatis, 4 rue Candolle, 5th, *T* 01 43 31 40 39. Delicious Greek eats to take away. *M* Censier-Daubenton.

Oliviers & Co, 128 rue Mouffetard, 5th, *T* 01 55 43 83 42. Everything to do with olives: oil, soap, bottles, and so on, nicely packaged. *M* Place-Monge

Quatrehomme, 118 rue Mouffetard, 5th, *T* 01 45 35 13 19. Delicious cheeses and wines. *M* Place-Monge

Rendez-vous de la nature, 96 rue Mouffetard, 5th, *T* 01 43 36 59 34. The largest range of health foods and organic products in Paris. Also beauty products. *M* Place-Monge

Les Saveurs du Panthéon, 200 rue St-Jacques, 5th, *T* 01 43 54 26 37. Homemade chocolates. *M* Luxembourg

HOMES

Games in Blue, 24 rue Monge, *T* 01 43 25 96 73. Board games, ancient and modern, wooden jigsaw puzzles and many other games. *M* Cardinal-Lemoine

La Porcelaine Blanche, 119 rue Monge, 5th, *T* 01 43 31 93 95. All white porcelain - cups, plates, bowls, etc. *M* Censier-Daubenton

La Route de la Soie et ses Merveilles, 14 rue Lacepède, 5th,
T 01 45 87 24 59. Furniture mainly from China, objects and silk
materials. *M* Place-Monge

La Tuile à Loup, 35 rue Daubenton, 5th, *T* 01 47 07 28 90. Traditional
French crafts in wood, pottery and wood, and specialist bookshop of
regional, ecological, ethnological works. *M* Censier-Daubenton

MUSIC

CD Choc, 15 rue Soufflot, 5th, *T* 01 56 24 46 47. Vast range of CDs which
can be listened to prior to purchase; also cassettes and videos, new
and second-hand. *M* Cluny-La Sorbonne, *RER* Luxembourg

Crocojazz, 64 rue de la Montagne-Ste-Geneviève, 5th, *T* 01 46 34 78 38.
Specialists in jazz and blues CDs. *M* Maubert-Mutualité

Jussieu Musique, 19 rue Linné, 5th, *T* 01 43 31 14 18. This branch
specializes in rock and pop CDs. The other four are: **Jussieu
Classique**, 16 rue Linné; **Jussieu Music World**, 20 rue Linné; **Jussieu
Jazz**, 5 rue Guy-de-la-Brasse; **Jussieu Musique Hip Hop**, 17 rue Guy-
de-la-Brasse. *M* Jussieu

Paris Jazz corner, 5 & 7 rue de Navarre, 5th, *T* 01 43 36 78 92. The place
to buy or sell jazz music. *M* Place-Monge

D'ORSAY
ST-GERMAIN

Musée d'Orsay

OPEN	Tues-Sat, summer 9.00-18.00, winter 10.00-18.00, Sun 10.00-18.00 all year; Thur until 21.15
CLOSED	Mon, 1/1, 1/5, 25/12
CHARGES	€7, reduced price €5 (for 18-25s and over-60s). Admission free for under 18s and, subscribers to the *Société des amis du Musée*, students of artistic curricula, recipients of certain social benefits (unemployed) as well as teachers and researchers, disabled visitors and carers, on presentation of valid proof of eligibility. Free access for all on the first Sunday of the month
TELEPHONE	01 40 49 48 48
WWW.	musee-orsay.fr
MAIN ENTRANCE	1 rue de la Légion d'Honneur, 6th
METRO	Solférino, **RER** Musée d'Orsay
DISABLED ACCESS	Plans for visitors with restricted mobility (from Information Desk) and wheelchair hire (from the Cloakroom)
PUBLICATIONS	*Plan-guide du Musée d'Orsay* and *Guide to the Musée d'Orsay*
AUDIO GUIDES	Available in English, €5
PHOTOGRAPHY	Hand-held cameras and camcorders may be used without flash or tripods
SHOP	Bookshop and boutique with gifts, postcards, posters, etc. Mailbox
EATING	**Restaurant du Palais d'Orsay** (Middle Level), with good food including an excellent-value buffet; also a salon de thé. **Café des Hauteurs** (Upper Level) for snacks and light meals

Unusually, for a national museum, open on Tuesdays. Musée d'Orsay holds frequent temporary exhibitions as well as concerts, films and lectures.

The Musée d'Orsay is best known for its outstanding collection of Impressionist works although its overall aim is to continue, chronologically, where the Louvre leaves off. National collections of the second half of the 19c and the early 20c were assembled here from the Louvre, the Jeu de Paume, the Palais de Tokyo, the Musée de Luxembourg and provincial museums, as well as through donation and acquisition. The works exhibited include all aspects of the visual arts: painting and drawing (including pastels), sculpture, decorative arts and photography, recording the different themes which run through Impressionism and beyond.

The main permanent collection - approximately 4700 paintings, 500 pastels, 2260 sculptures, 1300 objets d'art, and 45,000 photographs (exhibited in rotation) - is displayed over three floors. Separate sections are devoted to individual collections. On the forecourt of the museum are bronzes commissioned for the first Trocadero Palace built for the Paris Universal Exposition of 1878, and on rue de Lille are works of 1925 by Bourdelle.

At the time of writing, the museum is undergoing renovations which will cause disruption to some of the galleries until early 2004.

THE BUILDING

The building was originally a train station with a hotel attached, the Gare and Hôtel d'Orsay, built 1898-1900. The architect, Victor Laloux, designed it with a metal framework, intended to be both functional and decorative and to this end the Seine elevation was faced with stone to complement the Louvre on the opposite bank. By 1939 the station had virtually outlived its usefulness but the condemned building was saved by the belated revival of interest in the 1970s in the conservation of 19c industrial architecture, and the decision was then taken to convert it into a museum. The

Musée d'Orsay

architects chosen for the museum were Renaud Bardon, Pierre Colboc and Jean-Paul Philippon of ACT and the architect/designer responsible for the interior was Gae Aulenti. Certain rooms retain their original decoration of the 1900s. The magnificent new museum opened at the end of 1986.

The first impression of the interior is of space and light. The coffered vault - with its 1600 rosettes - of the central hall, which once spanned the platforms, is 138m in length, 40m wide and 32m high. The architects wanted to create a museum on a human scale without losing the original perspectives.

The installations use a great deal of pale polished Buxy stone and are designed neither to emulate nor to vie with the original building.

HIGHLIGHTS

Honoré Daumier's series of 36 painted clay caricatures of Parliamentarians	Room 4
Works by Gustav Courbet	Room 7
Early Manets	Room 14
Early works by Monet and Renoir	Room 18
The superb collection of Impressionist and Post-Impressionist art: Monet, Renoir, Van Gogh, Cézanne, Gauguin, Seurat, Rousseau and Toulouse-Lautrec	Rooms 29-48

GROUND FLOOR

CENTRAL AISLE In this section, watched over by the great clock, are displayed some of the more important sculptures by Rude, David d'Angers, Pradier, Préault and Barye. The 19c works come into their own in this large, lucid area where the drama of the marbles and bronzes contrasts with the severely geometric division of the lateral space.

On the left as you enter is one of the most extreme examples of Romanticism, albeit in a Classical guise: *Napoleon Awakening to*

MUSÉE D'ORSAY
Middle Level

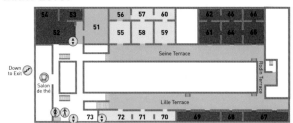

Upper Level

Ground Floor

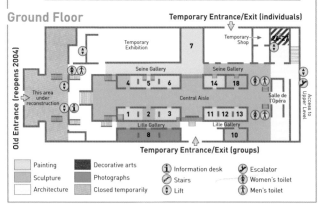

Immortality (1846), by François Rude, a plaster version of the monument made for Fixin in Burgundy, close to Dijon, birthplace of the sculptor. The creative energies of Jean-Baptiste Carpeaux can be fully appreciated in works such as the *Ugolin Group* (1862), the *Four Quarters of the World* bearing the celestial sphere (1867-72) for the fountain on Avenue de l'Observatoire, and *The Dance* (1869) commissioned for the façade of the Opéra Garnier. Facing the main aisle is a huge canvas by Thomas Couture, *Roman Decadence* (1847), much praised in its time. Works by **Rodin**, Camille Claudel, Bourdelle, Maillol and Joseph Bernard are on the terraces around the central aisle and other sculptures are scattered through the galleries (see below).

WORKS FROM THE PERIOD UP TO 1880 *Rooms 1-3* include two dominant yet contrasting painters and their followers, the Neoclassical **Jean Auguste Dominique Ingres** and the Romantic **Eugène Delacroix**. Representative of their works are Ingres' *La Source* (completed 1856) and Delacroix's *The Lion Hunt*. *The Tepidarium* (1853) by Théodore Chassériau - student of Ingres, admirer of Delacroix, and later the teacher of Moreau - was inspired by one of the thermae discovered at Pompeii. The technically competent but vacuous works of Salon painters such as Alexandre Cabanel and Winterhalter are also in this section.

LILLE GALLERY *Rooms 9-10* History paintings, portraits (1850-80) and temporary exhibitions.

ROOMS 11-13 The museum owns several important works by **Puvis de Chavannes**, who had a profound influence on many later painters including the Symbolists and Seurat. They include *The Poor Fisherman* (1881), and *The Pigeon* and *The Balloon*, the latter two painted during the Siege of Paris (1870-1). Close by are works by **Gustave Moreau**. Early (i.e. before 1870) works by **Edgar Degas** include the finely tuned family group, *The Bellelli Family* (1858/60); portraits of the artist's grandfather, painted on a visit to Italy in 1857; *The Orchestra of the Opéra* (1868/9) and the unfinished *Semiramis Watching the Construction of Babylon* (1861).

SEINE GALLERY AND ROOMS 4-6 Across the central aisle are works of the mid-19c which include not only paintings by **Honoré Daumier**, such as *The Laundrywoman* (c 1863), but also his remarkable series of 36 painted clay **caricature busts** of parliamentarians, modelled from 1831.

The paintings of the 1860s include Ernest Meissonier, *Campagne de France*, and pleasant but undemanding rural scenes by Jules Breton, Rosa Bonheur, Constant Troyon, Félix Diem, Eugène Isabey, early works by Delacroix, and small animal bronzes by Bayre. From this period are also the gentle silvery landscapes of **Jean-Baptiste Corot**; works by the Barbizon painters: Théodore Rousseau (1812-67), Charles Daubigny (1817-78), and Diaz de la Peña (1807-76), who paved the way for open-air painting; and the atmospheric and dignified canvases of **Jean-François Millet**, including *The Gleaners* (1857), *The Angelus* (1858/9) and several portraits and landscapes.

ROOM 7 The large and sometimes sombre works of **Gustave Courbet** were both controversial and influential. *The Burial at Ornans* was considered scandalous at the Salon of 1850 because of its blatant realism. Its counterpart, equally huge and impressive, *The Artist's Studio* (1855), depicts Baudelaire reading, on the right. The Orsay also owns Courbet's beautiful nude *The Origin of the World* (1866).

ROOM 14 On the right of the Seine gallery are works by **Edouard Manet** before 1870. This stunning group of paintings includes *Portraits of his Parents* (1860), *Lola de Valence* (1862), *Bullfight* (1865-6), *The Balcony* (c 1868-9), with Berthe Morisot in the foreground, the audaciously defiant *Olympia* (1863), and *Portrait of Zola* (1868), with the previous painting in the background. *The Fife-Player* (1866) contrasts the rigorous play of black and white with the red trousers of the musician. There are some delicious still lifes.

ROOM 18 Early works by **Claude Monet** are shown with pre-1870 works of his friends and colleagues, **Auguste Renoir** and Frédéric Bazille, and reveal the early experiments which led to

Impressionism. By Monet are *Portrait of Mme Gaudibert*, two sections from *Le Déjeuner sur l'herbe* (1865-6), *Women in a Garden*, painted in the open air, and *The Magpie*, the black and white bird pictured against the subtle whites of a snow-covered landscape. Here also are works executed before 1870 by Renoir, *Bazille Painting* (1867); and by Bazille, *Portrait of Renoir*.

ROOMS 15-17, 19-23 Many of these painters were close to the Impressionists or were their forerunners. Henri Fantin-Latour recorded the artistic milieu of the day in *The Studio in the Batignolles* (1870), showing Manet at the easel and grouped around him Monet, Bazille, Zola, Renoir and others; and in *A Corner of the Table* are the poets Verlaine and Rimbaud. There are also charming small marine paintings by Boudin, Lépine and Jongkind.

In the Antonin Personnaz collection are 14 landscapes by **Camille Pissarro** which date from 1870 to 1902: *Winter at Louveciennes* (c 1870) and green scenes such as *Landscape at Chaponval* (1880) and *Woman in an Enclosure* (1887) show the evolution of his later style. Also here are *Bridge at Argenteuil* (1874) by Monet, *The Place Valhubert* and *Paris, Quai de Bercy in the Snow* by Guillaumin, and *Woman Sewing* (c 1880-2) by Mary Cassatt, her only painting in the Orsay. The Eduardo Mollard collection includes *The Seine at Notre-Dame* by Jongkind, *Beach at Trouville* (1864), a well-known work by Boudin, and *The Bridge at Moret-sur-Loing* (1893) by Sisley.

Canvases by Adolphe Monticelli, who was admired by Van Gogh, and others are representative of the harsh light of Realism. Orientalism refers to paintings inspired mainly by North Africa and Egypt and in the footsteps of Ingres and Gérôme are Guillaumet's *Evening Prayer in the Sahara* (1863) and *The Desert* (1867).

OPERA ROOM The space below the main vault of the building is devoted to Charles Garnier and the construction of the Paris Opéra, started in 1862. This contains a maquette of the entire Opéra quarter at 1:100 as it was in 1914 (beneath a transparent floor); a model of the building shown as a cross-section; and a maquette of the stage built for the Universal Exhibition of 1900.

ROOMS 24-27BIS On the Seine side at the east end of the museum is Richard Peduzzi's *Architectural Tower*. Successive elevations of the tower demonstrate architectural features of public and private constructions of the period 1850-1900.

Stairs from this level take you up through the architectural plans and design section with maquettes and examples of furniture by designers such as Augustus Pugin, Philip Webb, Charles Rennie Mackintosh, Frank Lloyd Wright, Otto Wagner and Adolf Loos.

UPPER LEVEL

The escalators hidden behind the Opéra display take you up to the **Impressionist galleries**, a very popular and often crowded part of the museum.

ROOMS 29-34 The first gallery contains one of the most notorious picnics of all time, *Le Déjeuner sur l'Herbe* (1863) by **Manet**, which, 140 years later, manages through juxtapositions of flesh and fabric, voluptuous still life and abandoned blue dress to remain provocative. More demure is the all-time favourite by **Monet**, *The Poppies* (1873), a halcyon moment. 19c engineering features in *The Railway Bridge at Argenteuil* (c 1875). Nearby are Fantin-Latour's *Hommage to Delacroix*, Sisley's *The Footbridge at Argenteuil*, and works by Pissarro.

In the following galleries are James Whistler, *Arrangement in Grey and Black* (1871), an austere but harmonious composition featuring the artist's mother. Two tender interpretations by Berthe Morisot, *The Cradle* (1872) and *Young Woman in a Ball Gown* (1879), contrast with the vigorous *Floor Planers* (1875) by Gustave Caillebotte.

Among works by **Degas**, the moving portrayal of dejection in *The Absinthe Drinkers* (1876) and the fatigue of *Women Ironing* (c 1884-6) contrast with an altogether more lively glimpse of other worlds in *The Dancing Class* (1873-6) and *The Stock Exchange* (c 1878-9). His bronzes include the 14-year-old *Dancer wearing her tutu*. More

Vincent van Gogh *Self-Portrait* (1889-90)

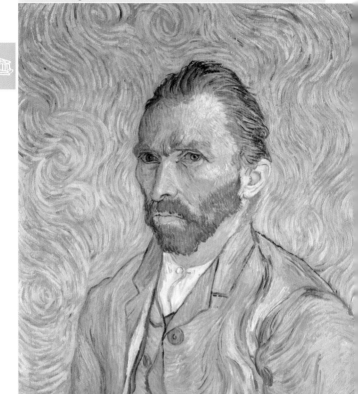

works by Manet are *On the Beach at Berck-sur-Mer* (1873), the marvellous *Lady with the Fans* (1873-4), and, at his most impressionistic, the portraits of *Mallarmé* and of *Clemenceau*.

Works before 1880 include Monet's *Regatta at Argenteuil* (c 1872), the *Fête in the Rue Montorgueil* (1878), and *St-Lazare Station* (1877). Landscapes by Pissarro include *Red Roofs*. The effects of dappled light are used by **Renoir** in paintings of 1876 such as *Dancing at the Moulin de la Galette* and *The Swing*; also, among his sculptures, are a bust of *Mme Renoir*.

Later Impressionist works by Monet include *Woman with the Sunshade* (1886), five of the series of views of the *Cathedral at Rouen* (1892-3), showing the effects of light at different times of day, and one example of the *Haystacks* series. By Renoir are the joyful *Dance in the Country*, and the more restrained *Dance in the Town* of 1883 and *Girls playing the Piano*.

ROOMS 35-38 In these rooms are a large number of the best-loved paintings by **Vincent van Gogh**. From the dark and brooding early paintings, his work erupts into the vigorous impasto and high colour of *The Portrait of Dr Paul Gachet* (1890), a portrait of the doctor who befriended the Impressionists and whose collection was donated to the museum. It includes Van Gogh's *Bedroom at Arles* (1889); two *Self-portraits*, of 1887 and 1889-90, electrifying in the use of colour and the tense energy of the brushstrokes; and the intense *Church at Auvers-sur-Oise* (1890).

The museum possesses a significant cross-section of the works of **Paul Cézanne**. From his earlier period is the *Portrait of Achille Emperaire* (1869/70), while examples of his monumental mature works include *The Card-players* and *Woman with a Coffee-pot*. Among the landscapes are the *Bay at Estaque* (c 1878-9), the *Bridge of Maincy* (1879), and *Mont Ste-Victoire* (c 1890); and gloriously coloured and textured still lifes such as the voluptuous *Apples and Oranges* (c 1899). *Bathers* (c 1890) was his last and largest canvas of male nudes.

Nearby are **Toulouse-Lautrec**'s panels for La Goulue's booth at the Foire du Trône, and later pastels by Degas.

The adjacent **Rooftop Café** provides a curious version of Paris through the hands of the huge clock, and panoramic views from the terrace.

ROOMS 39-44 These rooms contain the late works by **Monet** and **Renoir**. Monet's *The Houses of Parliament, London, Sunlight in the Fog* (1904), *Lily Pond* (1899 and 1900), and *Blue Waterlilies* (c 1916-8), and blue iris in *The Garden at Giverny* (1900). Renoir's *Large Bathers* (c 1918-9) is considered the culmination of his art.

Examples of Odilon Redon's mysterious and luminous pastels include *The Buddha* (1906/7), and there are also pastels by Ker-Xavier Roussel, Maurice Denis, and Georges Rouault.

At the western end of the museum is the Gachet collection, containing work by **Henri (le Douanier) Rousseau** such as *Portrait of a Woman* (c 1897) and the *Snake Charmer* (1907). Next are the Pont Aven painters, Emile Bernard, Paul Sérusier, and **Paul Gauguin**. Here are Gauguin's Brittany and South Seas periods (from 1875 to 1903), his style evolving from Impressionism to a flat decorative style with symbolic use of colour: *Washerwomen in Pont-Aven* (1886), *La belle Angèle* (1889); *Tahitian Women on the Beach* (1891), *And the Gold of their Bodies* (1901); *Self-Portraits* of 1893-4 and 1896.

ROOMS 45-48 Works from the 1890s are in the last rooms on this level. Neo-Impressionism or Pointillism, represented by **Georges Seurat** in his preparatory sketches for *La Grande Jatte*, and *The Circus* of 1890/91; Pointillism or Divisionism becomes coarser and richer in the hands of Paul Signac, Henri Cross and Maximilien Luce. **Henri Matisse** adapts the technique in *Luxe, Calme et Volupté* (1904) to shimmering horizontal dashes captured within an outline.

Further works by **Toulouse-Lautrec** include *Jane Avril Dancing* (c 1891), *La Toilette* (1896), and *Cha-U-Kao* (the female clown) (1895). Small format paintings by the Nabis (Symbolist painters who took their name from the Hebrew word for prophet), include Pierre Bonnard, Maurice Denis, Félix Vallotton and Edouard Vuillard.

ROOMS 49-50 There are pastels by Millet, Manet, Degas and Redon, and the Kaganovitch collection with Gauguin's,

Breton Peasant Women, and works by Monet, Sisley, Renoir, Van Gogh and others.

MIDDLE LEVEL

Escalators or stairs go down to the **Press Corridor**, which traces the development of images in the press over the period. The restaurant is on this Middle Level.

ROOM 51 The former ballroom or **Salle des Fêtes** of the station hotel, a prime example of the decorative arts of the Third Republic, has been restored to its former glitzy glory, with gilded mirrors and chandeliers. Large portraits of society beauties and frivolous paintings by William Bouguereau mingle with sleek statues by Denys Puech and Ernest Barrias.

SEINE TERRACE Monumental sculpture of 1870-1914, by Barrias, Coutain, Frémiet and Gérôme, mainly addresses themes of conflict, power or heroism; for example, Frémiet's *St Michael*.

ROOMS 55, 57-58 These galleries are devoted to Naturalism and Realism. Among them are paintings by Bastien-Lépage, Léon Bonnat, Jacques-Emile Blanche and Philip Wilson Steer, and Gérôme's bust of *Sarah Bernhardt* (c 1895).

ROOMS 59-60 Among the Symbolist works are Burne-Jones' *The Wheel of Fortune*; and paintings by Gustav Klimt, Edvard Munch and James Ensor.

ROOMS 61-66 A fascinating section containing **Art Nouveau** production from several European countries has jewellery by René Lalique; glass, ceramics and enamels by Emile Gallé and the School of Nancy, as well as Albert Dammouse; and stained glass by Louis Comfort Tiffany and Jacques Gruba. There are also examples, perfectly crafted and sometimes exquisitely over-the-top, of furniture and woodwork by craftsmen such as Hector Guimard; Alexandre Charpentier, with a dining room of 1901;

Louis Majorelle, with a bedroom suite entitled Nénuphars (c 1905); and Peter Behrens, with chairs of c 1902.

RODIN TERRACE Outside these rooms is an important collection of sculpture by **Auguste Rodin**, including his marble entitled *La Pensée*, of the head of Camille Claudel, and Claudel's own impressive bronze group *Maturity (L'Age Mûr)*.

LILLE TERRACE AND ROOMS 67-69 Recent acquisitions and temporary thematic exhibitions are held in the small galleries. A room devoted to civil decoration during the Third Republic has a series of sketches for the Panthéon friezes. Sculpture continues on the terrace with Emile-Antoine Bourdelle and Aristide Maillol.

ROOMS 70-72 Largely post-1900 paintings by the Nabis. The large canvas *Hommage à Cézanne*, by Denis, is a gathering of these painters around Cézanne's canvas *Compotier, Verre et Pomme*. There are large decorative panels by Edouard Vuillard, as well as the canvases *In bed* (1891) and *Portrait of Thadée Natanson*, and many of Pierre Bonnard's contributions show a heavy debt to Japanese art.

Among collections of **early photographs** (shown in rotation) are representative examples of the art of Eugène Atget, Edouard Baldus, L.-A. Humbert de Molard, Félix Nadar, Charles Beresford, Julia Margaret Cameron, Lewis Carroll, Roger Fenton and George Shaw.

Musée Rodin

OPEN	April–Sept 9.30–17.45, gardens until 18.45; Oct–March 9.30–16.45, gardens until 17.00
CLOSED	Mon, 1/1, 1/5, 25/12
CHARGES	€5, reduced price €3, garden only €1. Free admission for under 18s
TELEPHONE	**01 44 18 61 10, 01 44 18 61 10** (recorded)
WWW.	**musee-rodin.fr**
MAIN ENTRANCE	77 rue de Varenne
METRO	Varenne
DISABLED ACCESS	There are facilities for disabled visitors but only the ground floor is suitable for motorized wheelchairs. For the visually impaired, a hands-on visit of bronzes is possible
PUBLICATIONS	An introduction to the collection and information sheets in English are available in some rooms. *Tout l'Oeuvre*, published by the museum, is sold in the shop
AUDIO GUIDES	Available in English, €4
PHOTOGRAPHY	Hand-held cameras may be used without flash or tripods
SHOP	There is a bookshop/boutique open to non-ticket holders
EATING	**Le Jardin de Varenne**, a café in the gardens open to garden-only ticket holders

The Hôtel Biron, a stately 18c mansion in its gardens, provides an ideal setting for the important collection of works by Auguste Rodin, donated by the artist to the State in 1916. This much-loved museum contains many original marbles and bronzes, as well as plaster casts, maquettes, drawings and watercolours. It also houses his personal collection of art, antiquities and furniture, together with some 8000 old photographs associated with the sculptor. The museum mounts temporary exhibitions.

Hôtel Biron

   The collections comprise some 6600 works, and nearly 500 completed sculptures are on show in the museum, from all periods of his creative life (the remainder are at the museum in Meudon). The exhibits are on two floors, with the first few rooms arranged chronologically and the rest thematically. This presentation emphasizes the revolutionary nature of Rodin's art compared to academic sculpture at the time, as well as his debt to Michelangelo. He opened new vistas in sculpture in much the same way as the Impressionists did in painting, although he was not as vigorously criticized.

THE BUILDING

The Hôtel Biron was built in 1728-30 by Jean Aubert and Jacques-Ange Gabriel in Rococo style, and purchased by the Duc de Biron in 1753. At that time it had a fine interior décor of carved and gilded panelling. The house passed to Biron's heirs before being acquired by the aristocratic convent of the Sacré-Coeur in 1820, who removed much of the 'ostentatious' décor, and it served as a place of education for young ladies until 1904.

In 1905 the State acquired the house and rented out the rooms. Rodin was introduced to it by the poet Rainer Maria Rilke. In 1908 Rodin took four ground-floor rooms which he filled with works to present to guests, although his creative life continued at his home in Meudon. When the Hôtel was earmarked for demolition in 1908, the sculptor voiced his dream of creating his own museum there. However, its genesis was slow and finally opened in 1919, nearly two years after the Rodin's death.

HIGHLIGHTS

The Gates of Hell	Courtyard
The Age of Bronze	Room 3
The Kiss	Room 4
Works by Camille Claudel	Room 6
Paintings collected by Rodin	Room 14

FRONT COURTYARD

Several of Rodin's major commissions are
exhibited here, including the large group, the
Burghers of Calais (1889), the *Thinker* (1881), and
Balzac (1898). The *Gates of Hell* (1880-90) were
based on Ghiberti's Baptistery doors in Florence,
the iconography inspired by Dante's *Inferno*.
Intended for the Musée des Arts Decoratifs but
never installed they were, in fact, cast only in 1926.

The Thinker (1881)

GROUND FLOOR

ROOMS 1-2 The visit begins to the left, past the shop, in rooms
that have small and often pretty or ornamental works of the early
period (1860-80), including the charming *Young Woman with a
Flowered Hat* (c 1865), a masterly terracotta, and *Mignon* (1872),
based on Rose Beuret, Rodin's lifelong companion whom he
married in January 1917, only a few months before he died.

ROOM 3 An oval room with original 18c woodwork, it contains *The
Age of Bronze* (1875-6), his first freestanding male nude figure. A
soldier modelled for him, but its exceptional vitality and physical
presence, unlike other works of the time, caused critics to accuse
him of casting the figure from life. Rodin was infuriated and
insulted and yet, looking at it in the 21c, we see that the figure is
clearly exaggerated.

ROOMS 4-5 Rooms overlooking the garden concentrate on the
voluptuous and audacious sculptures of embracing couples
including a version of his best known work, *The Kiss* (1886), as well
as the well-known duos *Adam and Eve* and *Paolo and Francesca*
(1886). The remarkably vigorous, although without arms or head,
Walking Man (1877) was modelled on an Italian peasant and was a
preparatory work for *St John the Baptist* (1878). In 1875 Rodin
discovered the magic of Michelangelo first hand and never looked
back. Technically, he preferred to model in clay and employed
assistants to carve marble or stone after his maquettes. The

Musée Rodin Salle d'Eve

technique of leaving part of a work untouched developed during just such a process. In the case of **The Hand of God** (1898 and 1902) the emergent image symbolizes the act of the Creation.

ROOM 6 The gallery is devoted to **Camille Claudel**, Rodin's pupil whom he not only greatly admired artistically but loved intensely during a stormy nine-year relationship. After leaving him she deteriorated mentally and was finally committed to an asylum where she died 30 years after they parted. *La France* and *l'Aurore* are compositions he modelled on her, whereas her own exceptional talent as a sculptress is demonstrated in pieces such as *The Gossips*, and *The Wave* (1897-1902) in onyx and bronze.

ROOMS 7-8 The next two rooms concentrate on women, both in the symbolic sense, such as *Eve*, and in the real sense with portraits of *Eve Fairfax*, the suffragette, *Lady Sackville-West*, and *Mrs Potter-Palmer*, some of them souvenirs of Rodin's numerous amorous liaisons.

UPPER FLOOR
ROOMS 10-13 The *Gates of Hell* provided Rodin with a source of motifs such as the *Three Shades* (1889; on the staircase). The upper galleries contain studies for, and more variations on, the *Gates of Hell* and the *Burghers of Calais*.

In the rooms overlooking the garden are preparatory works for public monuments, including clothed and unclothed versions of *Balzac*, commissioned in 1891, 42 years after the writer's death. The final model so shocked the patrons that they refused to accept it, and it was not cast in bronze until 1926.

The sculptor's intellectual and political connections are reflected in the group of male busts of *Clemenceau*, *George Bernard Shaw*, *Gustav Mahler* and *Puvis de Chavannes*. In his later years he was inspired by dancers, including Isadora Duncan who at one time occupied studios in this building. Among the last works (1890-1905) is the gravity defying *Iris, Messenger of the Gods*, headless and leaping.

ROOM 14 Paintings collected by Rodin include three glorious works by **Van Gogh**: one of three versions of the *Portrait of Père Tanguy* (1887), *Les Moissoneurs* and *La Vue du Viaduc à Arles*; a *Female Nude* (c 1880) by Renoir, and Monet's *Paysage de Belle-Isle*.

GARDENS

The gardens, which can be visited independently, were remodelled in 1993. The formal layout, flanked by mature trees, perfectly offsets the elegant south façade of the museum. Rodin's sculptures in the garden include *Whistler's Muse*, *Cybele*, *Bastien Lepage*, *Claude Lorrain* and, in the pool, *Ugolino and his Children*.

on route

Assemblée Nationale, 126 rue de l'Université, 7th; visits Sat 10.00, 14.00, 15.00, except when the Assembly is sitting; *T* 01 40 63 64 80. The seat of the Chambre des Deputés, or French parliament, is in the Bourbon Palace built in 1728. *M* Assemblée-Nationale

Ecole Nationale des Beaux-Arts, 14 rue Bonaparte, 6th. The first great architectural school and school of fine arts where many celebrated 19c and 20c artists studied. Courtyard open term-time. *M* St-Germain

Hôtel de Matignon, 57 rue de Varenne, 7th. Protected by armed police, the home of France's Prime Minister was built by Courtonne in 1721. An outstanding mansion, it was altered in the 19c and has a large garden. *M* Varenne

Institut de France, 23 quai de Conti, 6th; guided visits at 15.00 on Sat, Sun, PH; *T* 01 44 41 44 41. This superb domed, semi-circular Baroque building (1643-61) houses the Institute which encompasses five academies established to protect the arts and sciences, including the Académie Française. *M* St-Michel-Notre-Dame

Les Invalides, esplanade des Invalides, 7th; 10.00-18.00 (1 Oct-31 March 10.00-17.00), church until 19.00, closed 1/1, 1/5, 1/11, 25/12; *T* 01 44 42 37 72. Founded by Louis XIV for wounded soliders, this magnificent building was built in 1671-1706 by Libéral Bruant and Jules Hardouin-Mansart. Encompasses the tomb of Napoléon I in the Dôme Church, the Musée de l'Armée and the Musée des Plans-Reliefs (models of fortified sites). *M* Invalides

Musée Bourdelle, 18 rue Antoine Bourdelle, 15th; 10.00-17.40, closed Mon and PH; *T* 01 49 54 73 73. Bronzes and plaster casts of the sculptor's monumental works in his former studio/apartment. *M* Montparnasse-Bienvenue

Musée Delacroix, 6 rue Furstenberg, 6th; 9.30-17.00; *T* 01 44 41 86 50. The painter's studio with memorabilia, small paintings, and a little garden. *M* St-Germain

Musée Hébert, 87 rue du Cherche-Midi, 6th; Wed-Mon 12.30-18.00, Sat-Sun 14.00-18.00, closed Tues, PH; *T* 01 42 22 23 82. Home of E. Hébert (1817-1908), painter of Italian landscapes and society portraits, and cousin of the writer Stendhal. *M* Sèvres-Babylone

Musée Maillol, 59/61 rue de Grenelle, 7th; 11.00-18.00, closed Tues; *T* 01 42 22 59 58. Small, elegant museum with bronzes and other works by the sculptor including some of his muse, Dina Vierny, whose private collection of naive, Post-Impressionist and Russian art is also on view. Café. *M* Rue-du-Bac

Musée Zadkine, 100bis rue d'Assas, 6th; 10.00-17.40, closed Mon and PH; *T* 01 55 42 77 20. Small house and garden crammed with the full-range of works of the Russian sculptor. *M* Vavin, Notre-Dame-des-Champs

St-Germain-des-Prés, blvd St-Germain, 6th. The church that gives its name to the quarter is one of the oldest in Paris with parts going back to 11c and 12c. Interior painted by Flandrin in the 19c, and some interesting monuments. *M* St-Germain

St-Sulpice, pl St-Sulpice, 6th. A masterpiece of severe classical French architecture, with colonnaded portico, a famous organ and frescoes by

Delacroix of *St-Michael Vanquishing the Devil*, *Jacob Wrestling with the Angel* and *Heliodorus Chased from the Temple* (1855-61). *M* St-Sulpice

Tour Eiffel, Champ de Mars, 7th, *T* 01 44 11 23 23. No need to point out Paris's most famous landmark since 1889. On the river end of the Champ de Mars, Gustav Eiffel's 276m high metal structure on three levels lifts you to the stars. Restaurants. Daily 9.30-23.00. *M* Bir-Hakeim, Trocadéro

commercial galleries

The greatest concentration of art galleries is in the *quartier* behind the Institut de France, between blvd St-Germain and the Seine. Many are in picturesque narrow streets such as rue de Seine, rue Jacob, rue des Beaux-Arts, rue du Bac, rue de l'Université.

Bac-St-Germain, 23 rue du Bac, 7th, *T* 01 40 20 44 80, www.brasilier.fr. This gallery concentrates on the figurative works on canvas and paper of André Brasilier, whose themes include horses and musical instruments; also other moderns. *M* Rue-du-Bac

Anisabelle Berès, 35 rue de Beaune and 25 quai Voltaire 7th, *T* 01 49 27 94 11. Founded in 1951 and specializing in traditional graphic arts of the extreme Orient and avant-garde French 19c and 20c. *M* Rue-du-Bac

Claude Bernard, 7 & 9 rue des Beaux-Arts, 6th, *T* 01 43 26 97 07, www.claude-bernard.com. Sells contemporary figurative art and sculpture; six exhibitions a year of artists such as Morandi, Giacometti, Bacon, Maurice. *M* Mabillon

Jeanne Bucher, 53 rue de Seine, 6th, *T* 01 44 41 69 65. Specialists in works outside the mainstream. Artists such as Bissière, Dubuffet, Amado, Rebeyrolle, de Staël, Viera da Silva, Yamamoto Wakako and Yang Jiechang. *M* Odéon, Mabillon

Carlin Gallery, 93 rue de Seine, 6th, *T* 01 44 07 39 54. Variety of ceramic objects designed by international contemporary creators such as Arroyave-Portela, David Roberts, Malcolm Martin and Gaynor Dowling. *M* Odéon, Mabillon

Lagerfield Gallery, 40 rue de Seine, 6th, *T* 01 55 42 75 50. Primary focus is photographic record of fashion; also fashions. *M* Mabillon

Lefebvre, 15 rue du Pré-aux-Clercs, 7th, *T* 01 45 48 18 13,
www.lefebvre-petrenko.com. 1920s to 50s decorative arts, photos
and sculpture. *M* Rue-du-Bac

Loft, 3bis rue des Beaux-Arts, 6th, *T* 01 46 33 18 90. Loft promotes young
talented artists and contemporary Chinese artists little known in France.
M St-Germain-des-Prés

Maeght, 42 rue du Bac, 7th, *T* 01 45 48 45 15, www.maeght.com. Opened
by Adrien Maeght in 1957 who carries on the long family tradition of art
publications and working with prestigious artists such as Chagall, Miró,
Giacometti, Raoul Ubac, Calder, Léger, Rebeyrolle. Also young
international artists using all media. Reproductions and bookshop.
M Rue-du-Bac

Minsky, 46 rue de l'Université, 7th, *T* 01 55 35 09 00, www.leonor-fini.com.
Deals exclusively in the works of Leonor Fini. *M* Rue-du-Bac

Patrice Trigano, 4bis rue des Beaux-Arts, 6th, *T* 01 46 34 15 01.
Specializes in Surrealism, post-war abstraction, Nouveau Réalisme and
Pop Art. Artists include Hartung, Lam, Villeglé, César and Skira.
M St-Germain-des-Prés

Georges-Philippe & Nathalie Vallois, 36 rue de Seine, 6th, *T* 01 46 34 61
07. An attractive gallery selling contemporary works. *M* Odéon, Mabillon

Dina Vierny, 36 rue Jacob, 6th, *T* 01 42 60 23 18. International
modernism and Russian artists such as Poliakoff, Yankelevsky and
Kabakov. *M* St-Germain-des-Prés

eating and drinking

In St-Germain you won't go hungry, with a multitude of eating
places ranging from elegant Art Nouveau to minimalist design,
and from the most sophisticated, and expensive, to basic
student bars.

AT THE MUSEUMS

MUSÉE D'ORSAY

€ **Café des Hauteurs** (Upper Level), for snacks and light meals, open 10.00-17.00, and to 21.00 on Thur. (Museum ticket holders only.)

€€ **Restaurant du Palais d'Orsay** (Middle Level), **T** 01 45 49 47 03 (no reservations); lunch 11.30-14.30, tea 15.30-17.40; Thur open for dinner until 21.00. (Museum ticket holders only.) A magnificent survival from the old railway station hotel, with original 1900 painted and gilded décor. Good food, including an excellent-value buffet. It serves as a Salon de thé as well. The queues can be long.

MUSÉE RODIN

Le Jardin de Varenne, in the gardens; April-Sept 9.30-17.45. Light meals and snacks. (Also open to holders of garden-only ticket.)

EIFFEL TOWER

€€ **Altitude 95**, 1st floor, **T** 01 45 55 20 04. Bit of a tourist dive, but fun to eat in the Eiffel in Zeppelin decor. The cooking is average quality and prices affordable, but the views are great - book early for a window table. Lunch €17.50, dinner €45.

€€€ **Jules Verne**, 2nd floor, South pillar, **T** 01 45 55 61 44. Reach giddy heights by combining spectacular views, luxury, excellent service and highly refined cuisine. Lunch €53, weekday dinner €110. **M** Bir-Hakeim, Trocadéro

MUSÉE MAILLOL

€ **Café** at 59/61 rue de Grenelle, 7th, **T** 01 42 22 59 58; same hours as the museum. Light lunches and snacks.

SURROUNDING AREA

€ **Cité Zen Café**, 73 rue de Seine, 6th, **T** 01 43 29 01 22. A Parisian version of a New York deli, offering pastrami sandwiches, vegetarian dishes, burgers and eggs benedict. (Also **Coffee St-Germain**, 5 rue Perronet, 7th.) **M** Odéon, Mabillon

Cuisine de Bar, 8 rue du Cherche-Midi, 6th, **T** 01 45 48 45 69. Great place for an inter-shop coffee or snack lunch. **M** Sèvres-Babylone, St-Sulpice

Emporio Armani Caffe, 149 blvd St-Germain, 6th, **T** 01 53 63 33 50. On the 1st floor facing the church of St-Germain (Armani contributed to the restoration of the windows) is a slick Italian café, ideal for lunch. **M** St-Germain-des-Prés

Le Palanquin, 12 rue Princesse, 6th, _T_ 01 43 29 77 66. An authentic and very good north Vietnamese restaurant. Menus €12 (lunch), and €20 (dinner weekdays). _M_ St-Germain-des-Prés, Mabillon

Tsukizi, 2bis rue des Ciseaux, 6th, _T_ 01 43 54 65 19. One of the oldest sushi bars in Paris. _M_ St-Germain-des-Prés

Le 20, 20 rue de Bellechasse, 7th, _T_ 01 47 05 11 11. Traditional bistrot with a zinc bar, traditional cooking and favourable prices. _M_ Solférino

Yen, 22 rue St-Benoit, 6th, _T_ 01 45 44 11 88. Japanese cooking in trendy, minimalist surroundings. Specializes in _sobas_ (buckwheat noodles). Also delicious tempura. _M_ St-Germain-des-Prés

€€ **Barroco**, 23 rue Mazarine, 6th, _T_ 01 43 26 40 24. The menu features South American and Southern European specialities. Pleasant surroundings on two floors; an interesting selection of dishes with generous helpings. _M_ Odéon

Le Bélier, Hôtel le Bélier, 13 rue des Beaux-Arts, 6th, _T_ 01 44 41 99 00. A small, smartly redecorated hotel, with bar and comfortable dining room with 19c décor for an intimate meal. Variation on traditional cooking. Lunch €22.50. _M_ St-Germain, Mabillon

Le Bistrot de Paris, 33 rue de Lille, 7th, _T_ 01 42 61 16 83. Handy for the Musée d'Orsay, this up-market bistrot is how cafés used to be - no frills, efficient friendly service, and well-cooked simple fare. _M_ Rue du Bac, Solférino

Brasserie Lipp, 151 blvd St-Germain, 6th, _T_ 01 45 48 53 91. This famous rendez-vous remains reassuringly unchanged. A great place to pop into for a drink or traditional brasserie fare, and you may glimpse a celeb. _M_ St-Germain-des-Prés

Brasserie Lutétia, Hôtel Lutétia, 23 rue de Sèvres, 6th, _T_ 01 49 54 46 76. This is a terribly grand and large hotel but the brasserie is very traditional with good, simple cooking which attracts the famous. Sunday brunch €38, menu at €34, and vegetarian menu. _M_ Sèvres-Babylone

Café des Délices, 87 rue d'Assas, 6th, _T_ 01 43 54 70 00. A chic place with very individual ideas from chef Gilles Choukroun who creates some way-out combinations which usually work and look wonderful. Menu €32, lunch €14. _M_ Vavin, Notre-Dame-des-Champs

La Calèche, 8 rue de Lille, 7th, _T_ 01 42 60 24 76. An old favourite, well-placed for the Orsay and the antique shops. The food is reliably good and not over expensive. _M_ Rue du Bac

Aux Charpentiers, 10 rue Mabillon, 6th, *T* 01 43 26 30 05. A good, traditional bistrot with mainly classic dishes, but some slightly more inventive. Menu €25, lunch menu €19. *M* St-Germain, St-Sulpice

Cherche-Midi, 22 rue du Cherche-Midi, 6th, *T* 01 45 48 27 44; open until 23.45. Fashionable little Italian bistrot, producing good, simple, affordable food. *M* Sèvres-Babylone

La Cigale, 11bis rue Chomel, 7th, *T* 01 45 48 87 87. A cosy and cheerful café where soufflés are available in all guises, and could be chosen for any course. But then the rest of the cooking is good, too. *M* Sèvres-Babylone

Dédicace Café, 7 rue St-Benoît, 6th, *T* 01 42 61 12 70. Fairly recently opened, it is one of the nicest brasseries in the *quartier*, pleasant, comfortable, with a literary slant, and modern, quality cooking. Menus €31.50 and €27. *M* St-Germain-des-Prés

L'Epi Dupin, 11 rue Dupin, 6th, *T* 01 42 22 64 56. This small place remains terribly popular with all Paris because the cooking is excellent and the prices reasonable. However, it is overcrowded and the tables are squashed together in the 'olde-worlde' décor. Two fixed-time sittings. Menus €30, and €20. *M* Sèvres-Babylone

Gaya Rive Gauche, 44 rue du Bac, 7th, *T* 01 45 44 73 73. Specializes in fish and seafood which is absolutely fresh, and cooked simply but impeccably. Menu €31 weekday lunch. *M* Rue-du-Bac

Le Grenelle de Peking, 124 rue de Grenelle, 7th, *T* 01 45 51 77 23. Good Chinese food in a pleasant setting. Menus €10.80 and €15 weekdays only. *M* Varenne, Solférino

Le Petit Tiberio, 132 rue du Bac, 7th, *T* 01 45 48 76 25; open 12.00-14.30, 19.00-22.30. Reasonably priced Italian cooking. *M* Rue-du-Bac

Tan Dinh, 60 rue de Verneuil, 7th, *T* 01 45 44 04 84. A classy Vietnamese restaurant with the best of that country's cooking combined with excellent French wine. *M* Solférino

€€€ L'Arpège, 84 rue de Varenne, *T* 01 45 51 47 33. Nothing if not adventurous, this remains one of the best *haute cuisine* addresses. For a time chef Alain Passard became exclusively vegetarian, but he has now resumed normal service with fish and meat dishes. Flavours are subtly blended, and the décor is refined. *M* Varenne

Hélène Darroze, 4 rue d'Assas, 6th, *T* 01 42 22 00 11. This is an up-market address for beautiful food with a southwestern France flavour (*foie gras, piment d'Espelette, gâteau basque*) where Hélène hails from and trained. Inventive, delicious, and professional. Lunch menus €26, €33, €60; dinner, *dégustations* (tasters) €50, gastronomic menus €89 and €110. *M* Sèvres-Babylone

BARS AND CAFÉS

Le Bar du Marché, 75 rue de Seine, 6th, *T* 01 43 26 55 15. The rendez-vous of locals, always packed, waiters in dungarees - all very *titi parisien*. *M* Odéon

Café de Flore, 172 blvd St-Germain, 6th, *T* 01 45 48 55 26. This is and always has been a hang-out for artists and writers. It is a great place to drop in at any time, for whatever reason. *M* St-Germain-des-Prés

Café de la Mairie, 8 pl St-Sulpice, 6th, *T* 01 43 26 67 82. Neighbourhood café with terrace for watching the world go by. *M* St-Sulpice

Comptoir des Canettes, 11 rue des Canettes, 6th, *T* 01 43 26 79 15. For years this was known as Chez Georges and has remained popular. Younger crowd meets downstairs. Some live music. *M* Mabillon

La Palette, 43 rue Seine, 6th, *T* 01 43 26 68 15. An old-style Parisian brasserie and bar in the arty quarter which has maintained it's early 20th century aura. *M* St-Gemain-des-Prés

shopping

Enduringly elegant St-Germain is now the ultra chic and trendy *quartier* for clothes and shoes. Long-time home to many retail stores, the mood has changed since top designers moved in from the Right Bank and the likes of Armani and Sonia Rykiel staked their claim near the legendary cafés and the ancient church of St-Germain-des-Prés. Antiquarians, art dealers and interior designers have for many decades inhabited the narrow, picturesque streets between the boulevard and the river, but they too have been joined by fashion and accessory boutiques, also found around place St-Sulpice, once the exclusive domain of religious shops.

ACCESSORIES

Corinne Zaquine, 38 rue de Grenelle, 7th, *T* 01 45 48 93 03. Sophisticated affordable millinery. *M* Rue du Bac

Hervé Chapelier, 1 rue du Vieux-Colombier, 6th, *T* 01 44 07 06 50. Smart nylon bags in gorgeous colours. *M* St-Sulpice

IT, 66 rue des Saints-Pères, 7th, *T* 01 45 49 31 78. Upmarket designer labelled accessories. *M* Rue du Bac

Liwan, 8 rue St-Sulpice, 6th, *T* 01 43 25 07 40. Exotic Arabic-inspired home design and fashion. *M* Odéon

Mandarina Duck, 51 rue Bonaparte, 6th, *T* 01 43 26 68 38. Wide range of very fashionable bags in modern materials. *M* Mabillon, St-Germain

Marie Mercié, 23 rue St-Sulpice, 6th, *T* 01 43 26 45 83. Stylish hats, practical hats, ready-to-wear or made-to-measure. *M* Odéon

Marion Lesage, 15 rue du Prés aux Clercs, 7th, *T* 01 45 48 32 06. Works of art by boutique owner, lifestyle pieces and simple clothes. *M* Rue du Bac

Woman, 4 rue de Grenelle, 6th. Nathalie Rykiel fashion and erotic playthings. *M* Sèvres-Babylone

ANTIQUES

Le Carré Rive Gauche, www.carrerivegauche.com, is a group of around 120 antiques shops and art galleries in the area defined by quai Voltaire, rue du Bac, rue de l'Université and rue des Sts-Pères, open Mon-Sat with an annual event in June. There are shops dealing in all periods and types of antique furniture, silverware, rugs, tapestries, and paintings. *M* St-Germain-des-Prés

BOOKS

La Chambre Claire, 14 rue St-Sulpice, 6th, *T* 01 46 34 04 31. Books on photography; also exhibitions. *M* Odéon

La Hune, 170 blvd St-Germain, 6th, *T* 01 45 48 35 85. Open until midnight, selling French and international books on art, art history and literature. *M* St-Germain

Tea & Tattered Pages, 24 rue Mayet, 6th, *T* 01 40 65 94 35. Second-hand English paperbacks and mini tea shop. *M* Duroc

Village Voice, 6 rue Princesse, 6th, *T* 01 46 33 36 47. Anglo-American bookshop; great selection, new and old; readings. *M* Mabillon

CLOTHES

Agnes B, 6 rue du Vieux Colombier, 6th, *T* 01 44 39 02 06. Epitome of wearable, stylish women's clothes; beauty products. Menswear at no. 12, *T* 01 45 49 02 05. *M* St-Sulpice

Anne Fontaine, 68/70 rue des St Pères, 7th, *T* 01 45 48 89 10. Designer of classic white shirts for women has moved into interesting modern designs. *M* St-Germain, Sèvres-Babylone

Atsuro Tayama, 81 rue des Saints-Pères, 6th, *T* 01 49 54 74 20. Young fashions by Japanese designer. *M* St-Germain

Burberry, 55 rue de Rennes, 6th, *T* 01 45 48 52 71. Burberry given an Italian work-over for the 21c. *M* Rennes

Christian Lacroix, 2-4 pl St-Sulpice, 6th, *T* 01 46 33 48 95. Archetypal French couturier's ready-to-wear and children's line. *M* St-Sulpice

Cop. Copine, 3 rue Montfaucon, 6th, *T* 01 42 34 70 26. French modern designs and fabrics at good prices. *M* Mabillon

L'Eclaireur, 24 rue de l'Echaudé, 6th, *T* 01 44 27 08 03. Designer avant-garde casual wear and accessories for men and women. (Also 4th.) *M* Mabillon

Emporio Armani, 149 blvd St-Germain, 6th, *T* 01 53 63 33 50. Elegant corner store ranging from fashion to CDs and upstairs the **Caffè** (light lunches, snacks). *M* St-Germain-des-Prés

Eric Bompard, 46 rue du Bac, 7th, *T* 01 42 84 04 36. Cashmeres in all colours, mixed with silk or cotton according to season. *M* Rue-du-Bac

Etienne Brunel, 70 rue des Sts-Pères, *T* 01 45 44 41 14. Funky, idyosyncratic, ready-to-wear or reasonable and rapid made-to-measure. *M* St-Germain, Sèvres-Babylone

Isabelle Marant, 1 rue Jacob, 6th, *T* 01 43 26 04 12. Well-known elegant, French designer of comfortable clothes. *M* St-Germain

Martine Sitbon, 13 rue de Grenelle, 7th, *T* 01 44 39 84 44. Elegant clothes and accessories. *M* St-Sulpice

Miu Miu, 16 rue de Grenelle, 7th, *T* 01 53 63 20 30. The not quite so expensive and very desirable Prada line. *M* St-Sulpice

Onward, 147 blvd St-Germain, 6th, *T* 01 55 42 77 55. Determinedly 'Left Bank' designer styles on three floors. *M* St-Germain

Prada, 5 rue de Grenelle, 6th, **T** 01 45 48 53 14. Sought-after Italian fashions, women's clothes and accessories. **M** St-Sulpice

Séverine Perraudin, 5 pl St-Sulpice, 6th, **T** 01 43 54 10 63. Sophisticated, stylish, and wearable clothes for women. **M** St-Sulpice

Sonia Rykiel, 175 blvd St-Germain, 7th, **T** 01 49 54 60 60. For the sophisticated 20 to 40+ Parisienne; colour, prints and rhinestones. (**Sonia Rykiel Homme**, 194 blvd St-Germain, **T** 01 45 44 83 19, **Sonia Rykiel enfant**, 6 rue de Grenelle), **M** St-Germain, Sèvres-Babylone

Thierry Mugler, 45 rue du Bac, **T** 01 45 44 44 44. Range of super outfits for sexy ladies and male sophisticates. **M** Rue du Bac

Vanessa Bruno, 25 rue St-Sulpice, 6th, **T** 01 43 54 41 04. Young trendy fashions. **M** Odéon, St-Sulpice

Versus, 64-66 rue des Saints-Pères, 7th, **T** 01 45 49 22 66. The younger version of Versace. **M** St-Germain, Sèvres-Babylone

Yves Saint Laurent Rive Gauche, 6 pl St-Sulpice, 6th, **T** 01 43 29 43 00, and menswear no. 12, **T** 01 43 26 84 40. Clothes for the seriously fashion-conscious man or woman. **M** St-Sulpice

DEPARTMENT STORE

Le Bon Marché, 22 rue de Sèvres, 7th, **T** 01 44 39 80 00. The only department store on the left bank is truly elegant and attractive. It sells clothes, fashion accessories, kitchenware and the rest. Antiques in Shop 2, **La Galerie des Antiquaires**. (See also Food.) **M** Sèvres-Babylone

FLOWERS

Au Nom de la Rose, 46 rue du Bac, **T** 01 42 22 08 09, and 4 rue du Tournon, 6th, **T** 01 46 34 10 64. Wonderful aromatic roses and rose-based gifts. **M** Rue du Bac, Odéon

Christian Tortu, 17 rue des Quatre-Vents **T** 01 56 81 00 24, and 6 Carrefour de l'Odéon, 6th, **T** 01 43 26 02 56. Leading florist; boutique for numerous related products. **M** Odéon

Olivier Pitou, 23 rue des Saints-Pères, 7th, **T** 01 49 27 97 49. Particularly lovely bouquets. **M** St-Germain, Sèvres-Babylone

FOOD

Barthélémy, 51 rue de Grenelle, 6th, **T** 01 45 48 56 75. Tues-Sat 7.00-19.30. Old and revered cheese merchant with mouth-watering array. **M** Rue du Bac

Boulangerie Poilâne, 8 rue du Cherche-Midi, 6th, *T* 01 45 48 42 59, open Mon-Sat 7.15-20.15. The byword for huge brown loaves baked in a wood-oven, sold in sections and delicious toasted. This is where it all started in 1932 (but bread is no longer baked here). *M* Sèvres-Babylone, St-Sulpice

Debauve & Gallais, 30 rue des Sts-Pères, 7th, *T* 01 45 48 54 67. Chocolate makers since 1800. *M* St-Germain

La Grande Epicerie, Bon Marché, 38 rue de Sèvres, 7th, *T* 01 44 39 81 00. Mouth-watering gourmet food including the ultimate in picnic goodies. *M* Sèvres-Babylone

J. Leblanc et fils, 6 rue Jacob, 6th, *T* 01 46 34 61 55. Specialist choice of oils (hazelnut, peanut, truffle, pistachio, etc), vinegar and mustards. *M* St-Germain

Pierre Hermé, 72 rue Bonaparte, 6th, *T* 01 43 54 47 77. Top-quality cake and pastry shop. *M* St-Sulpice

Street markets: **Rue de Buci**, 6th. A once lively street market (Mon-Sat, Sun morning) is much reduced but some gourmet charcuteries and patisseries have survived. *M* Odéon. **Blvd Raspail** has an organic market on Sun. *M* Sèvres-Babylone

HOMES

Christian Liaigre, 42 rue du Bac, 7th, *T* 01 53 63 33 66. The hottest of interior designers. *M* Rue du Bac

Conran Shop, 117 rue du Bac, 7th, *T* 01 42 84 10 01. English designs at affordable prices. *M* Rue-du-Bac

17 par Carole de Bona, 17 rue de Sèvres, 6th, *T* 01 42 86 98 28. Swimming pool turned store for beds and bedding. *M* Sèvres-Babylone

Etats de Siège, 1 quai Conti, 6th, *T* 01 43 29 31 60. Contemporary designer furniture; also temporary exhibitions. *M* Odéon

Au Fil du Temps, 33 rue de Grenelle, 7th, *T* 01 45 48 14 68. Fab clothing and furnishing fabrics. *M* Rue du Bac

Flamant, 8 rue Furstenberg and 8 rue de l'Abbaye, 6th, *T* 01 56 81 12 40. Store divided into small areas to display Belgian designed silverware, fabrics, furniture, kitchenware. Lunch/tea room. *M* St-Germain

Gallerie Robert Four, 8 rue des Saints-Pères, 7th, *T* 01 40 20 44 96. Aubusson tapestries and rugs, readymade or to order. *M* St-Germain

Greenage, 98 rue du Bac, 7th, *T* 01 42 84 37 37. Eco-sound items in material derived from wheat-husks. *M* Sèvres-Babylone

La Maison Ivre, 38 rue Jacob, 6th, *T* 01 42 60 01 85. Handcrafted pottery and ceramics from all over France. *M* St-Germain

Michel Frey, 1-2 rue Furstenberg, 6th, *T* 01 46 33 73 00. The top designer of beautiful but costly furnishing fabrics; accessories at no. 2bis, *T* 01 43 26 82 61. *M* St-Germain

Muji, 27 & 30 rue St-Sulpice, 6th, *T* 01 46 34 01 10. Popular Japanese designed household goods and clothes. Attractive and practical gifts. *M* Odéon, St-Sulpice

Palladio, 27 rue des St-Pères, 6th, *T* 01 40 15 09 15. Colourful Venetian glass shaped into glasses, lamps, and decorative objects. *M* St-Germain

Tai Ping, 30 rue des St Pères, 7th, *T* 01 42 22 96 54. Traditional and modern Chinese carpets incorporating unusual designs. *M* St-Germain

Xanadou, 10 rue St-Sulpice, 6th, *T* 01 43 26 73 43. Architect designed objects for the home. *M* St-Sulpice

JEWELLERY

Clio Blue, 16 rue du Cherche-Midi, 6th, *T* 01 42 22 37 36. Costume jewellery. *M* Sèvres-Babylone, St-Sulpice

Naïla de Monbrison, 6 rue de Bourgogne, 7th, *T* 01 47 05 11 15. The best in contemporary jewellery design. *M* Varenne

KIDS

Agnes B, 22 rue St-Sulpice, 6th, *T* 01 40 51 70 69. Children's collection. *M* St-Sulpice

Baby Dior, 252 blvd St-Germain, 7th, *T* 01 42 22 90 90. Designer bootees, rompers, and the rest, for babies and toddlers. *M* Solférino

Bonpoint, 42 rue de l'Université, 7th, *T* 01 41 20 10 54. Pretty outfits for privileged tots to teenagers. (**Bonpoint Fin de Séries**, 82 Rue de Grenelle, 7th, end of the range.) *M* St-Germain

Pom D'api, 28 rue du Four, 6th, *T* 01 45 48 39 31. Wide range of children's shoes. *M* St-Sulpice

Sonia Rykiel enfant (See Clothes)

LINGERIE

Ci Dessous, 48 rue du Four, 6th, *T* 01 42 84 25 31. Attractively well cut and well designed lingerie and swimwear. *M* Sèvres-Babylone

Capucine Puerari, 63 rue des Saints-Pères, 6th, *T* 01 42 22 14 09. Beautiful lingerie (B cup only), swimwear and women's clothes. *M* St-Germain, Sèvres-Babylone

Sabbia Rosa, 73 rue des Saints-Pères, 6th, *T* 01 45 48 88 37. Refined or sexy but always luscious underwear in vast range of colours. *M* St-Germain

La paresse en douce, 97 rue du Bac, 7th, *T* 01 42 22 64 10. Elegant underwear and night clothes mainly in white. *M* Rue-du-Bac

MUSIC

FNAC, 136 rue de Rennes, 6th, *T* 01 49 54 30 00. Records, CDs, computer accessories, books, etc. *M* St-Placide, Montparnasse-Bienvenue

PERFUME AND BEAUTY

Annick Goutal, 12 pl St-Sulpice, 6th, *T* 01 46 33 03 15. *Le dernier cri* in perfumery, beautifully presented gifts. *M* St-Sulpice

L'Artisan Parfumeur, 24 blvd Raspail, 7th, *T* 01 42 22 23 32. Scents and fragrances, candles and potpourri. *M* Rue du Bac

Editions de Parfums Fréderic Malle, 37 rue de Grenelle, 7th, *T* 01 42 22 77 22, www.editionsdeparfums.com. Modern and unusual boutique and scents; experience the fragrances from glass testers, not on your skin. *M* Rue du Bac

Maître Parfumeur, 84bis rue de Grenelle, 7th, *T* 01 45 44 61 57. Exquisite perfumes for men and women, created from natural essences - no synthetics. *M* Rue du Bac

Octée, 18 rue des Quatre-Vents, 6th, *T* 01 45 81 00 24. Fragrances identified by colour. *M* Odéon

Shu Uemura, 176 blvd St-Germain, 7th, *T* 01 45 48 02 55. High-quality range of cosmetics. *M* St-Germain

SHOES

Around **Carrefour de la place Rouge**, in **rues de Grenelle, du Four** and **du Cherche-Midi**, shoe shoppers will get high on the mind-blowing number of designer stores selling all ranges from ultra-funky squash-your-toes to fuddy-duddy. *M* Sèvres-Babylone, St-Sulpice

entertainment

INFORMATION
TICKETS
THEATRE, OPERA, DANCE
MUSIC
CABARETS
CLUBS AND DISCOS

INFORMATION

Pariscope and *l'Officiel des Spectacles* are published weekly and are on sale at newsstands. The most trendy weekly guide for the Parisian is *Zurban*. The Office de Tourisme de Paris, 127 av. des Champs-Elysées, is another source of information.

www.zurban.com

www.parisfranceguide.com gives general information in English

www.parissi.com is the Parisian website to nightclubs, bars, and music, in French

TICKETS

IN THE UK
Globaltickets (Edwards & Edwards), 1 Regent Street, London SW1Y 4XT, *T* 020 7014 8550

Michael Cooks' Ticket Finders, 35 Tottenham Street, London W12 4RT, *T* 020 7386 7815, www.ticket-finders.com

Allo France, Viewpoint, Basing View, Basingstoke RG21 4RG, *T* 0870 240 5903, www.allofrance.co.uk

Mission Impossible, 37 Marylebone Lane, London W1M 5FN, *T* 020 7486 1666

IN PARIS
Office de Tourisme de Paris, 127 av des Champs-Elysées, can supply tickets for most events

Agence Perrossier, 6 pl de la Madeleine, 8th, *T* 01 42 60 58 31,
F 01 42 60 14 83

FNAC Billetterie, *T* 08 92 68 36 22 (€0.33/min), www.fnac.fr, or at FNAC
Forums at 1 rue Pierre Lescot, 1st; 136 rue de Rennes, 6th; 74 av des
Champs-Elysées, 8th

Kiosques, half-price tickets on the day: 15 pl de la Madeleine, 8th;
Esplanade de la Tour Montparnasse, 14th

Kiosque Jeune, 91 blvd St-Michel, 5th, *T* 01 40 51 12 05

Sos Théâtre, 6 pl de la Madeleine, 8th, *T* 01 44 77 88 55, *F* 01 42 60 14 83

Spectaplus, 252 rue du Fbg St-Honoré, 8th, *T* 01 53 53 58 60,
F 01 53 53 58 61

Virgin-Megastore, Carrousel du Louvre, 1st and 52/60 av des Champs-
Elysées, 8th

THEATRE, OPERA, DANCE

Opéra-Comique, Salle Favart, pl Boïeldieu, 2nd, *T* 0825 00 00 58
(€0.15/min). *M* Richelieu-Drouot

Opéra National de Paris, Palais Garnier, 9th. *M* Opéra, and **Opéra
National de Paris, Bastille**, 12th. *M* Bastille. Information/bookings
T 08 36 69 78 68 (€0.33/min), and www.opera-de-paris.fr

Théâtre des Champs-Elysées, 15 av Montaigne, 8th, *T* 01 49 52 50 50,
F 01 49 52 07 41. *M* Franklin Roosevelt

Théâtre du Châtelet, 1st, *T* 01 40 28 28 40. *M* Châtelet

Théâtre de la Comédie-Française, pl André-Malraux, 1st, *T* 01 44 81 15 15.
M Palais Royal/Musée du Louvre

Théâtre National Populaire (TNP), Palais de Chaillot, 16th, *T* 01 53 65 30 00.
M Trocadéro

Théâtre de l'Odéon, pl Paul-Claudel, 6th, *T* 01 44 41 36 36. *M* Odéon

Théâtre de la Ville, pl du Châtelet, 4th, *T* 01 42 74 22 77. *M* Châtelet

MUSIC

Between May and September, free concerts take place in some
20 of the city's gardens. Information from the Paris Tourist Office
or the Information Office at the Mairie de Paris.

Church music and organ recitals are frequently held at such
churches as Notre-Dame, St-Eustache, St-Germain-des-Prés,

St-Louis des Invalides, St-Séverin, St-Sulpice, St-Roch, St-Clotilde, St-Etienne-du-Mont, Saint-Merri, Saint-Germain l'Auxerrois, Chapelle de la Sorbonne and La Madeleine.

See also Annual Events (p 170).

CLASSICAL

Cité de la Musique, 221 av Jean Jaurès, 19th, *T* 01 44 84 45 45, www.cit-musique.fr. *M* Porte-de-Pantin

Maison de l'ORTF (de la Radio), 116 av du Président-Kennedy, 16th, *T* 01 56 40 15 16. *M* Passy

Salle Gaveau, 45 rue La Boëtie, 8th, *T* 01 49 53 05 07. *M* St-Augustin

Salle Pleyel, 252 rue du Faubourg St-Honoré, 8th, *T* 01 45 61 53 00, *F* 01 45 61 46 87. *M* Ternes

Théâtre du Châtelet (see above)

Théâtre de la Ville (see above)

JAZZ

www.jazzvalley.com for information on jazz in the city

Le Bilboquet, 13 rue St-Benoît, 6th, *T* 01 45 48 81 84, www.jazzvalley.com/venue/bilboquet. Cosy club with traditional jazz and traditional crowd every night from 22.30. *M* Germain-des-Prés

Le Caveau de la Huchette, 5 rue de la Huchette, 5th, *T* 01 43 26 65 05. www.jazzvalley.com. Daily to 2.30; jazz, swing and retro charm. *M* St-Michel

Cité de la Musique (see above) has a wide variety of popular and jazz concerts. *M* Porte-de-Pantin

Duc des Lombards, 42 rue de Lombards, 1st, *T* 01 42 33 22 88, *F* 01 40 28 98 52. The cream of the French scene. *M* Châtelet, Les Halles

Méridien Etoile, Jazz Club Lionel Hampton, 81 blvd Gouvion-St-Cyr, 17th, *T* 01 40 68 30 42. Blues, big-band, etc. *M* Porte-Maillot

Méridien Montparnasse, 19 rue du Cdt Mouchotte, 14th, *T* 01 44 36 44 36. *M* Montparnasse-Bienvenue

New Morning, 7/9 rue des Petites Ecuries, 10th, *T* 01 45 23 51 41. Trendy and fashionable, for jazz, blues and soul. *M* Château-d'Eau

Petit Opportun, 15 rue des Lavandières-Ste-Opportune, 1st, *T* 01 42 36 01 36. Tues-Sun, live concerts from 22.30. *M* Châtelet

Petit Journal Montparnasse, 13 rue du Cdt Mouchotte, 14th,

T 01 43 21 56 70, www.jazzfrance.com/pjm. Spacious and luxurious, all types of jazz. *M* Montparnasse-Bienvenue

Petit Journal St-Michel, 71 blvd St-Michel, 5th, *T* 01 43 26 28 59, www.petitjournalsaintmichel.com. Jazz and swing all the way, 21.00-1.15, closed Sun. *M* Cluny-La Sorbonne

Le Sunset, 60 rue des Lombards, 1st, *T* 01 40 26 56 60, www.jazzvalley.com. Jazz every evening, 22.30-2.00. *M* Châtelet

Utopia Café Concert, 79 rue de l'Ouest, 14th, *T* 01 43 22 79 66. Small and friendly, blues club, open until 3.00. *M* Peméty

La Villa, 29 rue Jacob, 6th, *T* 01 43 26 60 00. Swish establishment with well-known performers. *M* St-Germain-des-Prés

CABARETS, DINNER SHOWS

Girlie shows for which Paris is famous, vary from 'artistically exotic or erotic' to grossly vulgar. Among the more up-market are:

Crazy Horse Saloon, 12 av George V, 8th, *T* 01 47 23 32 32, *F* 01 47 23 48 26, www.lecrazyhorseparis.com. Well-established club with a slick review; dinner in nearby restaurant an option. *M* Georges V

Lido, 116bis av des Champs-Elysées, 8th, *T* 01 40 76 56 10, *F* 01 45 61 19 41, www.lido.fr. A top-class show with dinner; less expensive after midnight without dinner. *M* George V

Moulin Rouge, 82 blvd Clichy, 18th, *T* 01 53 09 82 82, *F* 01 42 23 02 00, www.moulin-rouge.com. Inevitably features the cancan. *M* Blanche

Paradis Latin Cabaret, 28 rue du Cardinal-Lemoine, 5th, *T* 01 43 25 28 28, *F* 01 43 29 63 63, www.paradis-latin.com. Dinner and cabaret. *M* Cardinal Lemoine

CHANSONNIERS

Au Lapin Agile, 22 rue des Saules, 18th, *T* 01 42 82 95 06. In Montmartre, this is one of the most famous *chansonniers* (cabaret). Performances include informal revues or pithy political satire, for which a fairly thorough knowledge of the language and latest argot is needed. 21.00-2.00. Closed Mon. *M* Lamarck-Caulaincourt

CLUBS AND DISCOS

Les Bains, 7 rue du Bourg-l'Abbé, 3rd, *T* 01 48 87 01 80. The old public baths recreated as an up-market and fashionable nightclub for beautiful people. Dancing from midnight. *M* Etienne-Marcel

Le Baliser, 47 rue Beiges, 1st, *T* 0142 33 74 26. Wed-Sun. Small, dynamic club with West Indian music. *M* Les Halles

Bar Lutèce, Hotel Lutétia, 45 blvd Raspail, 6th, *T* 01 49 54 46 46. Designed by Sonia Rykiel. Live jazz Tues, Thur-Sat. *M* Sèvres-Babylone

Le Batofar, 11 quai François Mauriac, 13th, *T* 01 56 29 10 00. Authentic old lightship attracts the mixing of some of the best international DJs. Also a place to go on Sunday afternoon. *M* Quai de la Gare

Bus Palladium, 6 rue Fontaine, 9th, *T* 01 53 21 07 33. Always a good evening, especially for girls on Tuesdays. Rap, R&B and house. *M* Blanche, Pigalle

Le Concorde Atlantique, 23 quai Anatole-France, Port de Solférino, 7th, *T* 01 47 05 71 03. Disco on a magnificent barge and occasional impromptu sightseeing cruises. *M* Concorde

L'Elysée-Montmartre, 72 blvd Rochechouant, 18th, *T* 01 55 07 06 00. One of the most fashionable clubs with house music evenings and 70s and 80s music. *M* Anvers

L'Esplanade, 52 rue Fabert, 7th, *T* 01 47 05 38 80. This Costes Brothers' production pulls the laid-back glamorous crowd until 2.00. *M* Invalides

Latina Café, 114 av des Champs-Elysées, 8th, *T* 01 42 89 98 89. Huge, exciting night-spot (and restaurant) with hot dance floor for Cuban and Brazilian music; until 5.00. *M* Georges V

La Locomotive, 90 blvd de Clichy, 18th, *T* 08 36 69 69 28 (0.33/min). Three dance floors and three types of music - patronized by the very young. *M* Blanche

Man-Ray, 34 rue Marboeuf, 8th, *T* 01 56 88 36 36. Glittering array of names associated with this venture. Attracts the fashion-crowd. Franco-Asian menu. *M* Franklin-Roosevelt

Mezzanine, 62 rue Mazaine, 6th, *T* 01 53 10 19 99. Intimate but minimalist lounge bar-gallery of Alcazar where beautiful people meet for Latin-groove and funk, good DJs and cocktails. *M* Odéon

Nouveau Casino, 109 rue Oberkampf, 11th, *T* 01 43 57 57 40. One of Paris's newer trendy venues, with a mix of rock, pop and electro depending on the programme. *M* Parmentier

Le Pré, 4-6 rue du Four, 6th, *T* 01 40 46 93 22. Restaurant and bar, open until 5.00, decorated in startling colours and spherical shapes. *M* Mabillon

Pulp, 25 blvd Poissonnière, 2nd, *T* 01 40 26 01 93. French electro music. *M* Grands-Boulevards

The Queen, 102 av des Champs-Elysées, 8th, *T* 01 53 89 08 90. The famous gay club with nightly themes and mix nights. *M* Georges V

The Rex Club, 5 blvd Poissonnière, 2nd, *T* 01 42 36 10 96. Electronic music, club, techno, house and so on ... depends on the mixing. *M* Bonne-Nouvelle

Le Satellit Café, 44 rue de la Folie-Méricourt, 11th, *T* 01 47 00 48 87. World music concerts (Tues, Wed, Thur) and DJs (Fri, Sat). *M* Oberkampf

Le Scorp, 25 blvd Poissonnière, 2nd, *T* 01 40 26 28 30. One of Paris's best known gay clubs. *M* Bonne Nouvelle

Sitatunga, 28 rue Vavin, 6th, *T* 01 45 48 82 45. Piano bar, live music and DJ. Mon-Sat to 5.00. *M* Vavin

Le Slow Club, 130 rue de Rivoli, 1st, *T* 01 42 33 84 30. Sundays for hip-hop evenings, and R' n B' on Wednesday, and sometimes famous rappers. *M* Louvre

La Suite, 40 av Georges V, 8th, *T* 01 53 57 49 49. It's trendy, it's chic, it's an evening out with the in-crowd. *M* Georges V

Tantra Lounge, 23 rue Mouffetard, 5th, *T* 01 47 07 16 61. A new 'Salon aphrodisiaque' modelled on the smart right-bank clubs. Wafts of incense and cocktails such as Tantric Orgasm. *M* Censier-Daubenton, Monge

WAGG, 62 rue Mazarine, 6th, *T* 01 55 42 22 00. An intimate, underground club which is part of the Conran French empire. WAGG = Whiskey à Go-Go. UK house music, presented by Valéry B. *M* Odéon

Planning

TOURIST OFFICES
GETTING THERE
GETTING AROUND
MUSEUM & GALLERIES
OTHER ESSENTIALS
PLACES TO STAY
ART CALENDAR

TOURIST OFFICES ABROAD

The French Government tourist office supplies general information, including advice on travel and accommodation. There is a useful online reference guide, www.franceguide.com and holiday bookings www.fr-holidaystore.co.uk

CANADA

1981 Avenue McGill College, Suite 490, Montreal, Quebec H3A 2W9, *T* 514 876 9881, 514 845 4868, mfrance@attcanada.net

REPUBLIC OF IRELAND

30 Merrion Street, Upper 2, Dublin, *T* 1560 235 235 (€0.95/min), frenchtouristoffice@eircom.net

UK

Maison de la France, 178 Piccadilly, London W1V 9AL, *T* 09068 244 123 (75p/min), *F* 020 7493 6594, info.uk@franceguide.com

USA

444 Madison Av., 16th floor, New York, NY 10020, *T* 410 286 8310, *F* 212 838 7855, info@francetourism.com.

John Hancock Center, Suite 3214, 875 North Michigan Av., Chicago, Il. 60611-2819, *T* 312 751 7800, *F* 312 337 6339, info.chicago@franceguide.com

9454 Wilshire Blvd, Suite 715, Beverly Hills, Ca. 90212-2967, *T* 310 271 6665, *F* 310 276 2835, fgto@gte.net

1-2 Biscayne Tower, Suite 1750, 2 South Biscayne Blvd, Miami, Fl 33131, *T* 305 373 8177, *F* 305 373 5828, webmaster@franceguide.com

OFFICE DE TOURISME DE PARIS

The main tourist office is at 127 av des Champs-Elysées, 8th. Open daily 9.00-20.00 (November-March, Sunday and public holidays 11.00-18.00, closed 01/05). It offers hotel reservations (same day), bookings for exhibitions, shows, concerts, and sightseeing coaches/boats; free brochures and inexpensive booklets on hotels, restaurants, sightseeing and annual events; also currency exchange. Paris Museum Pass on sale (see p 158).

T 08 92 68 31 13 (€0.34 /min), *F* 01 49 52 53 00, www.paris-touristoffice.com. *M* Etoile

GETTING THERE
BY AIR

Paris has two international airports, Roissy-Charles de Gaulle (CDG), north of the capital, with two separate terminals; and Orly, to the south.

For both: *T* 08 36 68 15 15 (€0.33/min), www.adp.fr

Paris-Beauvais is used by Ryanair. This small airport is 70km northwest of Paris.

FROM CANADA
Air Canada, *T* 1 888 247 2262, www.aircanada.ca

FROM IRELAND
Aer Lingus, *T* 0818 365 000, www.aerlingus.com, Dublin to Paris
Air France to Paris CDG, and **Ryanair** to Paris-Beauvais

FROM THE UK
Air France, *T* 0845 359 1000, www.airfrance.co.uk
British Airways, *T* 0870 850 9850, *F* 01612 475 707, www.ba.com
British Midland, *T* 0870 6070 555, www.flybmi.com
Ryanair, *T* 0870 1569 569, www.ryanair.com

FROM THE USA
Air France, *T* 1 800 237 2747, www.airfrance.com/us
American, *T* 1 800 433 7300, www.aa.com
British Airways, *T* 1 800-AIRWAYS, www.ba.com/usa

Continental, *T* 1 800 231 0856, www.continental.com

Delta, *T* 1 800 241 4141, www.delta.com

Northwest, *T* 1 800 225 2525, www.nwa.com

Nouvelles Frontiers, *T* 1 800 677 0720, 310 670 7318, www.newfrontiers.com

United, *T* 1 800 538 2929, www.ual.com

AIRPORT TRANSFERS TO CITY CENTRE
Charles-de-Gaulle (CDG)
RER B to Gare du Nord, 5.44-0.11, every 8 mins

Roissybus to Rue Scribe, 5.45 to 23.00, every 15 mins, *T* 08 36 68 77 14 (€0.33/min)

Cars Air France to Porte Maillot/Arc de Triomphe, 5.45-23.00, every 15 mins, €10 single/€17 return; to Gare de Lyon, Gare de Montparnasse, 7.00-21.00, every 30 mins, €11.50 single/€19.55 return. *T* 01 41 56 89 00, www.cars-airfrance.com

Taxis approx. €38-42

Orly
RER C to Gare d'Austerlitz, 5.45-23.00, every 20 mins

Orlybus to Denfert-Rochereau, 6.00-23.30, every 15-20 mins

Orlyval, RER B+Val (from Orly-Sud) to Paris, 6.00-23.00, every 4 mins peak times, €8.75. *T* 08 36 68 77 14 (€0.33/min)

Cars Air France to Montparnasse/Les Invalides, 6.00-23.00, every 15 mins, *T* 01 41 56 89 00, www.cars-airfrance.com

Taxis approx. €46-54

Paris-Beauvais
A bus service links the airport at Paris-Beauvais to Port Maillot in Paris. It departs from the airport 20 mins after the arrival of each flight, takes around 1 hr, and costs €10. Tickets can be purchased at the airport. For the return flight, the buses leave from the coach station on blvd Pershing, behind the Palais des Congres (Porte Maillot), 2 hrs and 45 mins before the flight's departure.

BY TRAIN FROM THE UK
Eurostar offers easy, high-speed travel for foot passengers between London Waterloo (in 2 hrs 35 mins) or Ashford, Kent, and Paris Gare-du-Nord. *T* 0870 5186 186, www.eurostar.com

Eurotunnel carries passengers with cars from Folkestone to Calais (35 mins), *T* 08702 353 535, www.eurotunnel.com

Rail Europe Travel, 17 Piccadilly, London W1V 0BA, *T* 0870 5848 848, www.raileurope.co.uk, for European rail travel including Eurostar

BY SEA FROM THE UK
Hoverspeed Fast Ferries, *T* 0870 240 8070, www.hoverspeed.co.uk. 35 mins by Hovercraft, 50 mins by Seacat. Dover to Calais

P&O, *T* 08405 20 20 20, www.POferries.com. Dover to Calais

SeaFrance, *T* 08705 711 711, www.seafrance.com. Dover to Calais

BY COACH FROM THE UK
Eurolines National Express, 52 Grosvenor Gardens, London SW1W 0AU, *T* 020 7143 219, www.eurolines.co.uk

GETTING AROUND
Métro/RER/bus route maps are available free at métro stations.

Information in English, *T* 08 36 68 77 14, from 6.00-21.00 and www.ratp.fr

TICKETS AND TRAVEL PASSES
Tickets, valid on métro and bus routes, are available at all stations and in some tobacconists (*tabacs*). Individual tickets are €1.30 each; a carnet of ten tickets €9.30. By métro, the fare is the same for any distance on the main inner network including changes; tickets operate a turnstile and must be retained throughout the journey.

By bus, one ticket is needed per journey (no transfers) and must be punched at the start of the journey in to the small machine at the front of the bus. Don't punch multi-voyage passes.

Paris-Visite is a ticket for 1, 2, 3 or 5 consecutive days of unlimited travel by métro, RER, bus, and suburban SNCF trains in zones 1-3 (excluding airports) which includes reductions to many tourist sites in Paris. They are available at all stations, Paris Tourist Office and Paris airports; in Britain at the French Travel Centre, French Railways, Eurostar ticket desks at both terminals.

BY METRO

The métro (Métropolitan) operates between 5.30 and 0.30 throughout Paris. The 16 lines are identified by number and the names of the terminal stations, e.g. Ligne 1 runs between Chateau-de-Vincennes and Pont-de-Neuilly.

RER

The RER (Réseau Express Régional) is a fast over-ground network serving Paris and the Paris region which is linked to the métro.

BY BUS

Buses are a friendly, but inevitably slower, way to travel. However, you can see the city en route. They run daily 7.00-20.30 with a reduced service in the evenings between 20.30 and 0.30; some lines do not run on Sundays. Route maps are displayed at stops and inside the bus; each stop is easily identified as its name is on the stop itself. One-way streets may entail a modified return route.

The Balabus serves the main tourist sites between Bastille and La Défense on Sundays and public holidays, April-September; stops are marked Bb. The Montmartrobus runs between the Mairie du 18ème and Pigalle.

BY TAXI

Taxis can be hailed on the street or at taxi ranks (phone number at each rank). The tariffs (A, B, C) applying to Paris are displayed inside the vehicle: Tariff A between 7.00 and 19.00; Tariff B 19.00 to 7.00, Sundays and public holidays; Tariff C Sundays and public holidays outside Paris. A tip of about 10 per cent is recommended but not mandatory. Additional charges are made for luggage, pick up from railway terminals and a fourth adult passenger.

Complaints should be addressed to the Service des Taxis, Préfecture de Police, 36 rue des Morillons, 15th, *T* 01 55 76 20 00

MUSEUMS AND GALLERIES

For details of opening times to individual museums and monuments see the relevant pages in the Museums and Galleries and On Route sections. In general, national museums and monuments are closed on Tuesdays, and municipal museums are closed on Mondays; some museums have late openings; smaller ones may be closed at lunchtime.

Commercial galleries are usually open Tuesday-Saturday 10.30-19.00. Buy direct on the Contemporary French Art website, www.art-contemporaine.com.

THE MUSEUM PASS

La Carte Musées et Monuments allows direct entry to some 70 museums and monuments in and around Paris. It cuts out queuing to enter the most popular museums - they can be long at the Louvre - but doesn't allow access to temporary exhibitions. The pass can be obtained from the Office de Tourisme, participating museums, SNCF stations, main métro stations, and FNAC stores. It costs (consecutive days only):

1 day   - €15
3 days - €30
5 days - €45

OTHER ESSENTIALS
DISABLED TRAVELLERS

GETTING THERE
Some carriers offer special concessions but must be informed in advance.

Eurostar Wheelchair passengers can travel 1st class at 2nd class rates

Eurotunnel Disabled travellers may remain in their cars for the journey

Only a limited number of hotels have facilities for disabled visitors.

GETTING AROUND
Only métro Line 14 and the RER have disabled facilities. Logos in France in airports and other public places (depicting physical, mental, partial

sight/blindness, impaired hearing/deafness) guide disabled travellers and their carers to appropriate assistance.

www.destinationvitavie.com gives personalized advice on transport and particular destinations.

ADVICE IN THE UK
Holiday Care Information Unit, 7th Floor, Sunley House, 4 Bedford Park, Croydon, Surrey CR0 2AP, *T* 0845 124 9971, www.holidaycare.org.uk

RADAR, 12 City Forum, 250 City Road, London EC1 V8AF, *T* 020 7250 3222, www.radar.org.uk

ADVICE IN THE USA
Mobility International USA, PO Box 10767, Eugene, Oregon 97440, *T* 541 343 1284, www.miusa.org

Society for Accessible Travel and Hospitality, 347 Fifth Av., Suite 610, NY 10016, *T* 212 447 7284, www.sath.org

EMBASSIES AND CONSULATES
Australian Embassy, 4 rue Jean Rey, 15th, *T* 01 40 59 33 00

British Embassy, 35 rue du Fbg St-Honoré, 8th, *T* 01 44 51 31 00; British Consulate, 16 rue d'Anjou (Visa Office), near the Embassy, *T* 01 44 51 31 00; visas *T* 01 44 51 33 01/01 44 51 33 03; passports *T* 01 40 39 80 64

Canadian Embassy, 35 av Montaigne, 8th, *T* 01 44 43 29 00

Irish Consulate, 4 rue Rude, 16th, *T* 01 45 00 20 87

New Zealand Embassy, 7ter rue Léonard de Vinci, 16th, *T* 01 45 00 24 11

US Embassy, 2 av Gabriel, 8th, *T* 01 43 12 22 22

HEALTH
HOSPITALS WITH ENGLISH-SPEAKING STAFF
American Hospital, Neuilly, 63 blvd Victor-Hugo, 92202-Neuilly, *T* 01 46 41 25 25 *M* Porte-Maillot

Franco-British Hospital, 3 rue Barbès, 92300-Levallois-Perret, *T* 01 46 39 22 22. *M* Anatole France

LATE-OPENING CHEMISTS
British & American Pharmacy, 1 rue Auber, 9th, *T* 01 42 65 88 29, open until 20.00 and Sat. *M* Auber

Pharmacie Les Champs, 84 av des Champs-Elysées, *T* 01 45 62 02 41, open 24 hours, *M* George V

Pharmacie International, 5 pl Pigalle, 9th, *T* 01 48 78 38 12, to 1.00. *M* Pigalle

Pharmacie des Arts, 106 blvd du Montparnasse, *T* 01 43 35 44 88, to midnight. *M* Vavin

LOST/STOLEN CREDIT CARDS

Carte Bleue/Visa, *T* 01 45 67 84 84

Diner's Club, *T* 08 10 31 41 59

American Express, *T* 01 47 77 72 00

Mastercard Eurocard, *T* 01 45 67 53 53

LOST/STOLEN PROPERTY

Bureau des Objets Perdus, Préfecture de Police, 36 rue des Morillons, 15th, *T* 01 55 76 20 20 (open Mon, Wed, 8.30-17.00, Tues, Thur 8.30-20.00, Fri 8.30-17.30). *M* Convention

OPENING HOURS

Small shops (e.g. *tabacs, boulangeries*) and cafés open 7.30/8.00; lunch begins at 12 noon; dinner is eaten from 20.00 onwards. Fashion boutiques and commercial galleries open around 10.00, and stay open till 18.00/19.00 on weekday evenings; some stores in the Marais open on Sundays. Most food shops open Sunday mornings. Many boutiques, galleries and stores close on Mondays.

PUBLIC HOLIDAYS - JOURS FERIÉS

1 January (Jour de l'An)

Easter Monday (Pâques)

Whit Monday (Pentecôte)

Ascension Day (Ascension) 40 days after Easter Day

1 May, Labour Day (Fête de Travail)

8 May (end of World War II in Europe)

14 July, Bastille Day (Fête Nationale)

15 August, Assumption (Assomption)

1 November, All Saints' Day (Toussaint)

11 November (Armistice)

25 December, Christmas (Noël)

SIGHTSEEING
BY COACH
The following companies run tours with commentaries:

Cityrama, 4 pl des Pyramides, 1st, *T* 01 44 55 61 00, www.pariserve.com

Les Cars Rouges, 17 quai de Grenelle, 15th, *T* 01 53 95 39 53, www.lescarsrouges.com, hop-on-and-off service, ticket valid for 2 days

L'Opentour, 13 rue Auber, 9th, *T* 01 43 46 52 06, www.paris-opentour.com, open-top buses

Paris Vision, 214 rue de Rivoli, 1st, *T* 01 42 60 30 01, www.parisvision.com

Touringscope, 11bis blvd Haussmann, 9th, *T* 01 53 34 11 91, www.touringscope.com

BY BIKE (VÉLO)
Bullfrog Bike Tours, *T* 06 09 98 08 60, www.bullfrogbikes.com

Maison Roue Libre (RATP), *T* 01 53 46 43 77, www.ratp.fr

Paris Vélo c'est Sympa, *T* 01 48 87 60 01, www.parisvelosympa.com

BY BOAT
Batobus, *T* 01 44 11 33 99, www.batobus.com a river shuttle service (no commentary), operating beginning April-beginning Nov, with eight different stops along the Seine

The following companies operate river cruises with commentaries both during the day and after dark:

Les Bateaux-Mouches, Pont de l'Alma, 7th, *T* 01 42 25 96 10

Bateaux Parisiens/Seino Vision, quai Montebello pier (Notre-Dame), 5th, *T* 01 44 11 33 44, or Port de la Bourdonnais, 7th, *T* 01 44 11 33 44, operate April-Nov

Vedettes de Paris, Port de Suffren (Bir Hakeim), 7th, *T* 01 47 05 71 29; Vedettes du Pont-Neuf/Marina de Bercy, sq du Vert-Galant, Ile de la Cité, 1st, *T* 01 46 33 98 38

PLACES TO STAY

Hotels are officially classified by stars awarded by the French Tourist Board which refer to the comfort and service offered. The star system is only a rough guide to prices, which vary considerably within each category and according to season. High season is June, September and October; middle season is March, April, May, 1-15 July, November; low season is January, February, mid-July to end of August, and December. The price bands quoted here are for a twin/double room with en suite bath or shower and do not necessarily include breakfast. A tourist tax is charged on accommodation in Paris, ranging from €0.15 to €1 per person per night, and may either be included or added to the price quoted.

www.paris-touristoffice.com for information and online reservations

☆	Simple, with basic comfort, €60-85
☆☆	Comfortable, €80-130
☆☆☆	Very comfortable, €115-200
☆☆☆☆	High class, comfortable, €150-550
L☆☆☆☆	Very high class, de luxe, €350 and above

HOTELS

LOUVRE TUILERIES

☆☆   **Grand Hôtel du Palais Royal**, 4 rue de Valois, 1st, *T* 01 42 96 15 35, *F* 01 40 15 97 81. Part of a small chain, this non-swish hotel is close to Palais Royal and the Louvre, with a spacious lobby and corridors, and 82 recently-renovated and very clean, double-glazed rooms with parquet floors, shower or bath. Two rooms suitable for disabled visitors. Breakfast buffet/caféteria on the ground floor. Prices include tax and reductions can be negotiated for small groups. Single €108, double/triple €118-134, breakfast €8. *M* Palais Royal-Musée du Louvre, *RER* Châtelet-Les-Halles

Londres St-Honoré, 13 rue St-Roch, 1st, *T* 01 42 60 15 62, *F* 01 42 60 16 00, hotel.londres.st-honore@gofornet.com. This and the St-Roch (see below) are friendly, family run establishments, ideally placed for the Louvre, Opéra Garnier, the Tuileries and shopping in rue St-Honoré. Bargain prices for the area and neat, light rooms. €84-100, triple/suite €112-200, breakfast €6.50. *M* Tuileries, Pyramides, *RER* Châtelet-Les-Halles

St-Roch, 25 rue St-Roch, 1st, **T** 01 42 60 17 91, **F** 01 42 61 34 06, hotel.st-roch@gofornet.com. Same ownership as the Londres St-Honoré above; some airy, bright rooms under the eaves. Prices as above. **M** Tuileries, Pyramides, **RER** Auber

☆☆☆ **Brighton**, 218 rue de Rivoli, 1st, **T** 01 47 03 61 61, **F** 01 42 60 41 78, hotel.brighton@wanadoo.fr. www.esprit-de-france.com. An affordable hotel facing the Tuileries Gardens and close to Place Vendôme. Part of the small group Esprit de France, it aims to combine comfort and creativity. Some of the 39 rooms have been recently renovated and it is worth asking for one of these when you book; those benefiting from views of the gardens are on busy rue de Rivoli. Single €115-155, double/twin €115-226, triple €164-252, breakfast €8. **M** Tuileries. **RER** Châtelet-les-Halles

☆☆☆☆ **François Ier**, 7 rue Magellan, 8th, **T** 01 47 23 44 04, **F** 01 47 23 93 43, hotel@hotel-francois1er.fr, www.the-paris-hotel.com. A smallish, luxury hotel conveniently close to the Champs-Elysées, and situated in a quiet street. Ideal for a special occasion visit. Close to shops, bars and restaurants, with elegant lobby and bar and tea room. The richly decorated bedrooms are a good size, and although the bathrooms are not huge they are well thought out. Single/double €290-460, suites €580-640; breakfast €21. **M** Georges-V, **RER** Charles-de-Gaulle-Etoile.

Louvre, 1 pl André Malraux, 1st, **T** 01 44 58 38 38, **F** 01 44 58 38 01, sales-hoteldulouvre@concorde-hotels.com, www.hoteldulouvre.com. This is a grand affair belonging to the Concorde chain. The 130 sizeable rooms are individually designed with views over the Louvre, the Comédie Française, Opéra Garnier or Palais Royal. The painter Camille Pissarro lived here and a suite is named after him. There is an elegant bar and a typically Parisian brasserie-style restaurant with terrace-eating in the summer. Rooms €450-1100, breakfast €21. **M** Palais Royal-Musée du Louvre, **RER** Auber

BEAUBOURG MARAIS

☆☆ **Place des Vosges**, 12 rue de Birague, 4th, **T** 01 42 72 60 46, **F** 01 42 72 02 64, hotel.place.des.vosges@gofornet.com. This small hotel is ideally situated for the Marais, and is close to Ile St-Louis. Some rooms are being done up in Louis XIII style, and showers with massage-jets are being installed. The prices will increase correspondingly. Single €120-160, double €160-200. **M** Bastille, St-Paul, Sully-Morland, **RER** Gare-de-Lyon

★★★ **Duminy-Vendôme**, 3-5 rue du Mont-Thabor, 1st, *T* 01 42 60 32 80, *F* 01 42 96 07 83, dv@duminy-vendome.com. Built in the 19C, this centrally placed hotel between rue de Rivoli and rue St-Honoré is just round the corner from place Vendôme. It has 78 medium-sized rooms, attractively decorated with standard accessories, including tea/coffee making equipment in the larger ones. There is a bar, small courtyard, and a basement breakfast room. Two rooms are suitable for old-style wheelchairs (not modern electric ones). Competitive prices which vary according to season. Single €115-135, double/twin €150-225, breakfast €13. *M* Tuileries, *RER* Châtelet-Les-Halles

Bourg-Tibourg, 19 rue du Bourg-Tibourg, 4th, *T* 01 42 78 47 39, *F* 01 40 29 07 00, hotel.du.bourg.tibourg@wanadoo.fr, www.hoteldubourgtibourg.com. The celebrated designer Jacques Garcia is responsible for the neo-Viollet-le-Duc look (neo-Gothic/Oriental/Victorian) in this luxurious hotel. No surface is ignored and no detail spared. The smallish, warmly coloured rooms are luxurious and beautifully appointed with superb touches such as fringed lampshades and mosaic tiles in the bathrooms. The whole effect is slightly over the top. Single €150, double/twin €200-350 (no seasonal variations), breakfast €12. *M* St-Paul, Hôtel de Ville

La Bretonnerie, 22 rue Ste-Croix-de-la-Bretonnerie, 4th, *T* 01 48 87 77 63, *F* 01 42 77 26 78, hotel@bretonnerie.com, www.bretonnerie.com. This is a very charming hotel deep in the Marais with a pretty entrance hall and fine 17C staircase. Although the old building does not allow for spacious rooms, each of the 22 rooms and 7 suites is individually decorated in rich colours and fine fabrics contrasting with exposed beams and stone walls. The furniture is carefully chosen and includes some four-poster beds. Vaulted lower-ground floor breakfast room. Singles/doubles/suites €145-230, breakfast €9.50. *M* Hôtel-de-Ville

Tonic Hotel Louvre, 12-14 rue du Roule, 1st, *T* 01 42 33 00 71, *F* 01 40 26 06 86, Tonic.Louvre@wanadoo.fr, www.Tonichotel.com. Popular hotel in a prime position close to the Louvre, the quays of the Seine, and Beaubourg. Good, functional uncluttered rooms with the added bonus of the hydro-massage and steam bath in each bathroom, as well as competitive prices. Single €136, double/triple €151-183, breakfast €10. *M* Châtelet, *RER* Les Halles

☆☆☆☆ **Caron de Beaumarchais**, 12 rue Vieille-du-Temple, 4th, *T* 01 42 72 34 12, *F* 01 42 72 34 63, hotel@carondebeaumarchais.com, www.carondebeaumarchais.com. A quaint and delightful hotel decorated in an 18c style appropriate to the age of the building and its namesake, who was living at no. 47 when he wrote *Le Mariage de Figaro*. The shop-front style façade opens onto a lobby resembling a period room, with pianoforte, chandeliers, original gaming table, and a fireplace that is used on winter evenings. You'll be warmly greeted on arrival by the father and son team, Etienne and Alain Bigeard. Despite the authentic 300-year-old character of the 19 daintily presented rooms, they are all equipped with modern amenities. Double €137-152, breakfast (in rooms) €9.80. *M* Hôtel-de-Ville, St-Paul, *RER* Châtelet-Les-Halles

Ducs d'Anjou, 1 rue Ste-Opportune, 1st, *T* 01 42 36 92 24, *F* 01 42 36 16 63, ducs.danjou@wanadoo.fr, www.hotelducsdanjou.fr. Very close to the Beaubourg and Châtelet, this small hotel has recently been totally renovated and added a star to its rating. The rooms are bright, cheerful and not over-fussy, and the top-floor rooms under the eaves have views of the roofs of Paris. The prices are good and there is an attractive breakfast room in the stone-vaulted cellar. Single €100-150, double/suites €115-250, breakfast €12. *M* Châtelet, *RER* Châtelet-Les-Halles

☆☆☆☆ **Saint-Merry**, 78 rue de la Verrerie, 4th, *T* 01 42 78 14 15, *F* 01 40 29 06 82, hotelstmerry@wanadoo.fr, www.hotelmarais.com. Uniquely picturesque, this hotel occupies a former presbytery tucked under St-Merry in the Beaubourg; room 9 has a couple of buttresses flying over the bed. The medieval character is relentlessly and successfully enhanced by mock-Gothic furnishings, exposed beams, narrow staircase (no lift), reception on the first floor, and the absence of televisions (except in the only suite). Great position. Double/twin/suite €160-407, breakfast €11. *M* Châtelet/Hôtel de Ville, *RER* Châtelet-Les-Halles

LEFT BANK ST-MICHEL

☆ **Esmerelda**, 4 rue St-Julien-le-Pauvre, 5th, *T* 01 43 54 19 20, *F* 01 40 52 00 68. The most famous one-star hotel in Paris, in the Latin Quarter, has a miniscule entrance, a colourful clientele and shared showers for the cheaper rooms. Plus points are the rooms with a view over the Seine to Notre Dame, and the budget prices. Singles €30-60, doubles/triples €60-85. *M* St-Michel, *RER* St-Michel-Notre-Dame

★★ **La Sorbonne**, 6 rue Victor Cousin, 5th, *T* 01 43 54 58 08, *F* 01 40 51 05 18, reservation@hotelsorbonne.com, www.hotelsorbonne.com. Located in the university area, Boule Mich and the Luxembourg Gardens are on the doorstep. This inexpensive hotel (by Paris standards) is decorated with an excess of a rather curious green, but the rooms are adequate and clean, although small. All have shower or bath, TV, hairdryer. Single €80-90, double €80-90, breakfast €5. *M* Cluny-La Sorbonne, *RER* Luxembourg

★★★ **Notre-Dame 'Maître Albert'**, 19 rue Maître Albert, 5th, *T* 01 43 16 79 00, *F* 01 46 33 50 11, hotel.denotredame@libertysurf.fr. www.france-hotel-guide.com/h75005notredame.htm. On the Left Bank, this quiet hotel is across the Seine from the Ile St-Louis and Notre-Dame. The entrance lobby is enhanced with antiques and a tapestry, and the rooms are individually styled. There is a sauna and small fitness area available. Single €139-154, double/twin €139-154 (reductions out of season), breakfast €7. *M* Maubert-Mutualité, St-Michel, *RER* St-Michel-Notre-Dame

St-Paul, 43 rue Monsieur-le-Prince, 6th, *T* 01 43 26 98 64, *F* 01 46 34 58 60, hotel.saint.paul@wanadoo.fr, www.hotelsaintpaulparis.com. In an attractive area of St-Michel, a few steps from the Luxembourg Gardens, this British run hotel offers simplicity and good prices with pretty, small but well-equipped rooms (8 are air-conditioned). The welcome is warm and the 17c building is set off to advantage. Single €112-128, double/twin/suite €128-204; breakfast: continental €10, American €13. *M* Odéon, *RER* St-Michel-Notre-Dame

Select Hotel, 1 pl de la Sorbonne, 5th, *T* 01 46 34 14 80, *F* 01 46 34 51 79, Select.Hotel@wanadoo.fr, www.selecthotel.fr. Attractively situated in the Quartier Latin next to the Chapelle de la Sorbonne, it is a stone's throw to the Panthéon and the Musée du Moyen Age. The décor is refreshingly modern with a small atrium and interior garden in the entrance, although the vaulted breakfast room is a reminder of the old quarter. The rooms are quiet and some combine contemporary fittings with old stone. Competitive prices. Single €132, double/twin €149- 202, continental breakfast €6. *M* Cluny-La-Sorbonne, *RER* Luxembourg

★★★★ **Jeu de Paume**, 54 rue St-Louis-en-l'Ile, 4th, *T* 01 43 26 14 18, *F* 01 40 46 02 76, info@jeudepaumehotel.com, www.hotelduJeudePaume.com. A former real tennis court built at the time of Louis XIII is at the core of a 17c building on the Ile St-Louis which has been successfully and artfully converted into an unusual hotel. The island between the Marais and the Quartier Latin seems hardly touched since the 18c, not even a metro station, but there is a choice of restaurants and bars. The hotel is peaceful and secluded with a small garden courtyard (but no river views). Much is made of the timber-framework of the original building in the attractive public areas, while the bedrooms are tastefully presented in fresh, pale colours and include some split-level apartments (duplexes) overlooking the garden and two suites (the singles tend to be small). Single €152, double/twin/suite €210- 450, breakfast €14. **M** Pont-Marie, **RER** St-Michel-Notre-Dame

Meliá Colbert Boutique, 7 rue de l'Hôtel Colbert, 5th, **T** 01 56 81 19 00, **F** 01 56 81 19 02, melia.colbert@solmelia.com, www.solmelia.com. This is tucked away behind St-Julien-le-Pauvre deep in the Latin Quarter, a few steps from the Seine and Notre-Dame. The 'Boutique' hotels are the Meliá group's smaller establishments. This one has 39 rooms of great refinement, Single/double/twin €320-390, triple €549, suite €549-602; continental breakfast €15.50, buffet breakfast €24. **M** St-Michel, Maubert-Mutualité, **RER** St-Michel-Notre-Dame

Panthéon, 41 rue des Ecoles, 5th, **T** 01 53 10 95 95, **F** 01 53 10 95 96, pantheon@leshotelsdeparis.com, www.leshotelsdeparis.com. This is a serious hotel, sleek and shining, almost next door to the Musée du Moyen Age. It has been renovated recently in *style Ecossais* (Scottish style), incorporating leather Chesterfields and polished wood against dark greens and reds. The lobby is very smart with a large bar and interior garden. The less expensive rooms are not vast but they are all beautifully turned out and fully equipped. Prices vary greatly according to seasons. Single €180-280, double/twin/suite €200-410. **M** Cluny-La Sorbonne

D'ORSAY ST-GERMAIN

☆☆ **Hotel Bonaparte**, 61 rue Bonaparte, 6th, **T** 01 43 26 97 37 or 01 43 26 54 10, **F** 01 46 33 57 67. Just off place St-Sulpice, this simple hotel is good value and well positioned for shops, clubs and the Left Bank in general. The air-conditioned rooms are surprisingly attractive, with original fireplaces and mouldings. All have bath/shower. Single €84-131, double/twin €115-146. **M** St-Germain-de-Prés, St-Sulpice, Mabillon, **RER** Luxembourg

Hotel Recamier, 3bis pl. St-Sulpice, 6th, **T** 01 43 26 04 89, **F** 01 46 33 27 73. Close to St-Germain and the Luxembourg

gardens, situated in a quiet corner of a large square bordered with fashionable shops. Light, pleasant rooms, some quite spacious and some with views on to the church. Shared shower for lower priced rooms. Single €70-125, double/twin €85-130.
M St-Sulpice, **RER** Luxembourg

Hotel de la Tulipe, 33 rue Malar, 7th, **T** 01 45 51 67 21, **F** 01 47 53 96 37, hoteldelatulipe@wanadoo.fr, www.hoteldelatulipe.com. This small, cheerful hotel, in the shadow of the Eiffel Tower and close to lively shopping streets, has a Provençal feel. Once a convent, the building is arranged around a small interior courtyard. Sunny yellow fabrics contrast with old beams and stone walls. The rooms are well equipped and reasonably priced. Single/double €100-150, apartment €220-240; breakfast €9.
M Invalides, **RER** Pont de l'Alma

★★★ **Aviatic**, 105 rue de Vaugirard, 6th, **T** 01 53 63 25 50, **F** 01 53 63 25 55, welcome@aviatic.fr, www.aviatic.fr. Very close to Montparnasse and all that that area has to offer is this highly recommended and welcoming hotel. The tastefully simple lobby resembles the entrance to a private dwelling, with antique furniture, fine fabrics, and attention to detail. The breakfast room near the entrance (very good buffet) is lined with old posters. The rooms, with excellent bathrooms, are comfortable and stylish. Single €130-170, double/twin/triple €130-220, breakfast €12.
M Montparnasse-Bienvenue, **RER** Denfert-Rochereau

Fleurie, 32-34 rue Grégoire-de-Tours, 6th, **T** 01 53 73 70 00, **F** 01 53 73 70 20, bonjour@hotel-de-fleurie.fr, www.hotel-de-fleurie.fr. Described as home-from-home, this family-run hotel inhabits a charming 18c building which is surrounded by the famous cafés and designer shops of St-Germain. The public areas and bedrooms are restful and elegant, successfully combining old and modern. Single €130-145, double/twin/suite €165-325; breakfast buffet €10. **M** Mabillon, Odéon, **RER** St-Michel-Notre-Dame

★★★ **Lenox**, 9 rue de l'Université, 7th, **T** 01 42 96 10 95, **F** 01 42 61 52 83, hotel@lenoxsaintgermain.com, www.lenoxsaintgermain.com. The new theme at this old literary hotel is Art Deco leather upholstery and polished wood. The Lenox Club bar features marquetry images of jazz musicians. A glass elevator takes you to thoughtfully presented smallish bedrooms, with unusual duplexes under the eaves. Double/twin/suites €115-270, continental breakfast in room €10, buffet €12.50. **M** St-Germain-des-Prés, **RER** Musée d'Orsay

St-Germain-des-Prés, 36 rue Bonaparte, 6th, *T* 01 43 26 00 19, *F* 01 40 46 83 63, Hotel-Saint-Germain-des-Pres@wanadoo.fr, www.hotel-st-ger.com. A few yards from the church of St-Germain-des-Prés, a *quartier* bursting with shops and restaurants, is this exclusive little hotel in an 18C building. The individual character of each of the 30 comfortable rooms is accentuated by the hand-painted doors and variety of pretty flowery chintzes. The less expensive rooms in these old buildings tend to be small, but all are well-equipped and have good bathrooms. Double/twin/suite €150-305. *M* St-Germain-des-Prés, Mabillon, *RER* St-Michel-Notre-Dame

Univers, 6 rue Grégoire-de-Tours, 6th, *T* 01 43 29 37 00, *F* 01 40 51 06 45, GrandhotelUnivers@wanadoo.fr, www.hotel-paris-univers.com. Sister hotel to the St-Germain above, the original wooden beams and stone walls are a distinctive feature of the old building, part of which is reputed to be 15c. There is a spacious lobby and bar, the breakfast room has been created out of the vaulted cellar, and the rooms are lavishly decorated using fine fabrics in individual colour schemes. Its location between St-Germain and St-Michel allows easy access to the Seine and Ile de la Cité, shops and museums. Single €138-152, double/twin €154-185, continental breakfast €6.50, buffet breakfast €9.50. *M* Odéon, *RER* St-Michel-Notre-Dame

Verneuil, 8 rue de Verneuil, 7th, *T* 01 42 60 82 14, *F* 01 42 61 40 38, hotelverneuil@wanadoo.fr, www.hotelverneuil.com. A charming hotel situated close to St-Germain and the Musée d'Orsay in a 17C building. The rooms are small but interesting, with good bathrooms. Prices are very competitive. Single €120, double/twin €140-185; breakfast €12. *M* St-Germain-des-Prés, Rue du Bac, *RER* St-Michel-Notre-Dame

☆☆☆☆ **Buci**, 22 rue Buci, 6th, *T* 01 55 42 74 74, *F* 01 55 42 74 44, hotelbuci@wanadoo.fr, www.hotelbuci.fr. This is a charming hotel in the heart of St-Germain with high-quality service. It occupies a 16c building and has been totally renovated in good taste with a very attractive entrance lobby, bar and vaulted breakfast room. No detail is spared in the decoration of the bedrooms, which are a good size. All have elegant marble bathrooms. Single €165-237, double/twin €190-550, breakfast continental €15, buffet €20. *M* St-Germain-des- Prés, *RER* St-Michel-Notre-Dame

Lutetia, 46 blvd Raspail, 6th, *T* 01 49 54 46 46, 01 49 54 46 10, *F* 01 49 54 46 00, lutetia-paris@lutetia-paris.com, www.lutetia-paris.com. A seriously grand 1930s' style hotel with huge lobby, piano bar (jazz certain evenings), gastronomic restaurant and brasserie. All of the 250 spacious bedrooms and suites (one suite contains works by the artist Arman) are fresh from a recent refurbishment; hotel facilities include a fitness centre. Well placed for Montparnasse and St-Germain in an excellent shopping area just opposite Bon Marché. Single/double/twin €400-530, suites €650-1350, suite Arman €2300, breakfast €16. **M** Sèvres-Babylon, *RER* Montparnasse

ART CALENDAR
ANNUAL EVENTS
MAY
Ateliers d'Artistes de Belleville Artists' studios open throughout the Belleville quarter, *T* 01 46 36 44 09, www.ateliers-artistes-belleville.org

Atelier des Frigos 13th, www.lesfrigos.free.fr. Artists' squat in a former fridge factory May and November

JUNE
Fête de la Musique A national festival of music with all types of free concerts and music (professional and amateur) in a variety of venues. www.fetedelamusique.culture.fr

Amazing objets d'art, Carré Rive Gauche Festival in group of about 120 art galleries and antique shops, *T* 01 42 60 70 07, www.carrerivegauche.com

SEPTEMBER

Les Journées Europennées du Patrimoine Monuments, museums, châteaux and churches - even the Hôtel de Ville - which are usually closed are open to the public for two days and a night, *T* 01 56 06 50 21, www.jp.culture.fr

SEPTEMBER/OCTOBER
Festival d'automne Contemporary arts: dance, theatre, music, cinema and exhibitions, www.festival-automne.com

OCTOBER
Nuit Blanche The strangest night of the year, early in October, closes the summer season. This unique artistic night-time journey across the

capital includes music, video, contemporary creation, and so on, in well-known and unknown places. **T** 08 20 00 75 75 (€0.15 /min)

Ateliers de Ménilmontant Artists' studios open in the Ménilmontant district. 40-42 rue des Pandaux, 20th, **T** 01 46 36 47 17, www.artotal.com/menil **M** Ménilmontant, Père Lachaise

NOVEMBER
Les Journées des métiers d'Art An occasion to meet craftspeople in their workshops, to take part in animations and demonstrations in all types of decoration and art, **T** 01 55 78 85 97

ALL YEAR
Viaduc des Arts The brick arcades of the old railway viaduct are occupied by arts and crafts boutiques. 9-129 av Daumesnil, 12th, **T** 01 44 75 80 66. **M** Bastille

Pont Alexandre III

art glossary

Art Brut The term, invented by the artist Jean Dubuffet (1901-85), is described as Outsider Art in English and applies to art produced by those who have no formal training and are often on the margins of society. There are examples of Art Brut at the Pompidou Centre.

Art Deco A term coined in Paris after an exhibition of decorative and industrial art in 1925. Bold geometric shapes, rounded and streamlined are the hallmark of Robert Mallet-Stevens' (1886-1945) stylish Parisian buildings (see rue Robert Mallet-Stevens, 16th). An offshoot of International Modern, evocative of the Jazz Age, it was the fashionable style of ocean liners and skyscrapers.

Art Nouveau Its sinuous vegetal forms and arabesques spread into architectural and interior design throughout Europe and North America at the end of the 19c until World War I. Named after a Parisian shop of 1895 specializing in 'modern' goods, Art Nouveau synthesized earlier influences - Medieval, Celtic, the English Arts and Crafts Movement. The style was used for the first métro station entrances of 1900 (those surviving were restored in 2000). The Musée d'Orsay has a section devoted to Art Nouveau interior design including examples of the extravagant glassware shaped by Emile Gallé from Nancy.

Arte Povera An Italian expression which was used in 1967 by the critic Germano Celant to cover a bewildering range of conceptual or minimalist art. It utilizes poor or worthless materials, such as torn newspapers and organic waste to create another reality, thus liberating artists from conventional materials. Among exponents are Carl Andre, Joseph Beuys and Mario Mertz.

Aulenti, Gae (Gaetana) (b. 1927) The Italian architect commissioned to design the interior of the Musée d'Orsay, the museum created from a train station which was designed by Victor Laloux and began service in 1900. Aulenti's flexible and open space is deliberately detached from any visual references to Laloux's monument. She remodelled the Contemporary Art Gallery at the Centre Pompidou in 1985.

Baroque During the 17c and 18c painting, sculpture and architecture came together in a spectacle of illusionism, dramatic lighting, shocking realism and grand perspectives. Baroque developed in the south of Europe at the beginning of the 17c, during the Counter-Reformation, to intensify the emotional propaganda of the Catholic Church. Michelangelo, Caravaggio and Bernini were great Italian exponents. Rubens was the most important Baroque painter of the north, while the principal French Baroque architect was Louis Le Vau (1612-70) who built the Hotel Lambert on the Ile St-Louis and the Château of Vaux-le-Vicomte in the Ile de France.

Claude Gellée or **Le Lorraine** (1600-82) The antidote to Poussin, Claude's paintings are heavy in atmosphere and colour, composed to draw the eye into the deep beyond. Strong chiaroscuro and romantic landscapes or seascapes with elements of antique architecture are the setting for poetic visions of mythologial events. There are several works by Claude in the Louvre.

Dada One of the early revolts against traditional values in art and an expression of disillusionment following World War I, involving anarchic group activity which mocked established criteria of style and materialism. It began in Switzerland c 1915 and spread to New York. Leading members were the poet Tristan Tzara (1896-1963) and artists Jean Arp and Hans Richter.

Delacroix, Eugène (1789-1863) The major painter of the Romantic Movement in France who broke away from the classicizing constraints of Jacques Louis David, admired Rubens and Veronese, and was a fan of English painters, especially Constable. He was also inspired by British writers such as Byron, Shakespeare and Scott. A visit to North Africa in 1832 opened his eyes to exotic colour and culture. His works can be seen in the Louvre, in St-Sulpice, and his studio may be visited. Many later artists were influenced by Delacroix's handling of paint and use of colour.

David, Jacques Louis (1748-1825) Famous Neoclassical painter and excellent teacher, he was a deeply political figure who was considered at the time to be both a revolutionary and an opportunist who attached himself to the party of the day. His *Oath*

of the Horatii (1785, Louvre) made his reputation as an 'appeal to republican virtues and sentiments' although it was commissioned for the Crown. **Brutus** (1788, Louvre), on the other hand, was deliberately chosen to illustrate republicanism prior to the Revolution. He became a strong Bonapartist and produced overtly propagandist works for the Emperor, including the **Coronation of Napoléon at Notre-Dame** (Louvre 1804-7). Whatever the message, David's paintings are tremendously strong and vital.

Eiffel, Gustav (1832-1923) Most famous for the Tour Eiffel, built for the Paris Exhibiton of 1889 and at the time a radical and controversial building - at 923m it was also the tallest structure in the world. A tapering lattice-work tower, it is composed of 18,000 pieces of metal. Although Eiffel owned the construction firm which built it, the chief designers were engineers Maurice Koechlin and Emile Nougueir and the architect was Stephen Sauvestre. Another of Eiffel's metal structures is the Bon Marché department store on rue de Sèvres.

Expressionism As a movement, this developed from the 1880s in Germany. In a wider context, it describes a heightened sense of emotion and passion on the part of the artist. This intensity is most commonly expressed through the use of non-naturalistic colour. In this Vincent van Gogh (1853-90) led the way, and in France it was expanded on by the Fauves, by artists such as Vlaminck (see p 63). Concurrently the De Brücke and then the Blaue Reiter Groups in Germany were exploring the same sensations, as was the Norwegian Edvard Munch. The Pompidou Centre has many examples.

Futurism This avant-garde literary movement, celebrating the modern world of speed and violence and attacking etablished values, was almost entirely confined to Italy. Although most of its adherents were artists, it expanded to encompass all the arts and politics. Its wealthy founder Marinetti published the Futurist Manifesto on the front page of the French newpaper *Le Figaro* in 1909.

Gothic The medieval style of architecture which used rib vaults and flying buttresses to build churches to a great height and allowed the insertion of huge stained-glass windows in the non-load-bearing walls. Its beginnings are identified with the cathedral of St-Denis on the edge of Paris, c 1140, and it was the predominant style, with regional variations, throughout Europe until the early 15c. Gothic also describes the art of the period. The description was first used pejoratively by the Italian painter Vasari (1511-74). In the 19c admiration for all things medieval inspired a neo-Gothic revival.

Haussmann, Baron Eugène-Georges (1809-91) In 1853 Napoleon III made him Préfet de la Seine, with the authority to overhaul the city. Following on from urban improvements begun during the Age of Enlightenment (18c), Haussmann transformed Paris from a medieval slum to a city of grand boulevards and vistas. The great thoroughfare named after him was begun in 1857 and completed in 1926. It stretched from blvd Montmartre to the Arc de Triomphe and obliterated many small streets and buildings. Haussmann also enlarged place du Parvis Notre-Dame on the Ile de la Cité. The concept of urban planning on a grand scale, especially at the expense of medieval quarters, is often referred to as Haussmannism.

Impressionism The Impressionist movement took its name from Monet's *An Impression, Sunrise* (1874; Marmottan Museum, 16th) and was used derisively by a critic at the first Impressionist exhibition in Paris in 1874. Impressionist painters worked in the open air and sought to attain a convincingly naturalistic effect of a fleeting moment. Deeply attracted to the play of light on a subject, they attempted to emulate this by using small patches of paint. They were strongly influenced by the research into colour harmony and contrasts by the chemist Eugène Chevreul, such as optical mixing and simultaneous contrasts. The lightening of the palette (no black) and the liberation of colour from a purely natural palette by painters such as Monet, Pissarro and Sisley was the jumping off point for future artists. Pointillism, Divisionism, Neo-Impressionism and Post-Impressionism were the direct descendants of Impressionism.

Labrouste, Henri (1801-75) Best known for his pioneering use of wrought iron, the architect Labrouste was responsible for the construction of the domed Main Reading Room (1857-73) at the

Bibliothèque Nationale de France, Richelieu; his earlier wrought- and cast-iron structure is the Bibliothèque Ste-Geneviève (1844-50).

Maillol, Aristide (1861-1944) A sculptor whose works provides a counterpoint to that of the slightly older Rodin. Focussing on the female form, he preferred monumental, simple volumetric shapes to Rodin's more dynamic representations. His work can be seen in the Tuileries Gardens as well as at the museum dedicated to him which presents the scope of his talent and is the collection of his last muse, Dina Vierny.

Manet, Edouard (1832-83) After reacting violently against the Salon art of Couture's studio where he studied, Manet turned to subjects from contemporary life. Strongly influenced by Velázquez, Goya and Frans Hals, and Spanish subjects, his work is characterized by strong contrasts, especially black and white, with few half-tones. There is a superb collection of his work at the Musée d'Orsay, including two works which were considered scandalous at the time, *Déjeuner sur l'Herbe* and *Olympia*.

Mansart, François (1598-1666) Born in Paris, he was the first great interpreter of classicism in French architecture in a style which combines subtlety and ingenuity. A difficult character, reckless and intolerant, he was nevertheless fully confident in his own ability. Although involved with several projects in Paris there are few still standing. He designed the centrally planned church of Ste Marie de la Visitation (1632-4), near place de la Nation (12th), and remodelled the Hotel Carnavalet in 1660-1, his latest surviving work. The most complete work still extant is the Château of Maisons Lafitte outside Paris. The mansard roof - a hipped double roof, the lower section longer and steeper than the upper - is named after him.

Marais, The This colourful and historic district of Paris, between the Bastille and the Pompidou Centre, is so-called because it was built on marshland or *marais*. It was inhabited from the 13c by the Knights Templars and other religious institutions who converted the marshes into arable land. In the 17c it became a fashionable place to live.

Matisse, Henri (1869-1954) Matisse's concern with colour began when he was a pupil of Gustav Moreau and it developed under the influence of Impressionism and the light of the south of France. In association with painters such as Derain, Vlaminck and Signac he became leader of the Fauve movement, characterized by an arbitrary, non-naturalistic use of vivid colour. Around this time the American Stein family supported him, as did the Russian collectors Morosov and Sergei Shchukin. He was later deeply affected by Middle Eastern and North African art, and odalisques (a female slave in a harem) became a favourite motif. He also travelled to the South Seas. Interiors, models and decorative flat patterns were the subjects of his work in Nice in the 1920s. His 'cut-outs' were a means of sculpting in colour, and he used this technique for the designs of the Barnes Murals and the Dominican Chapel in Vence. There are some representative examples of his earlier work at the Musée d'Orsay, and later ones at the Pompidou Centre.

Mitterand, François (1916-86) Active in the Resistance during the World War II, he first stood as presidential candidate for the Left in 1965 and was faced with a run-off against General de Gaulle who won the day. Mitterand was finally elected President in May 1981 and held the post until his death in 1986. He was responsible for a number of fundamental reforms, such as decentralization, nationalization, and fiscal and legal reforms. During his leadership Paris was endowed with a number of *grands projets*, notably the improvements to the Louvre.

Monet, Claude (1840-1926) The leading Impressionist and the most dedicated to its aesthetics. To the end he was master of the visual sensation and of the changes in light and mood on a motif. In his Rouen series of (1891-5) the solid forms seem to dissolve into colour. He was deeply impressed by Japanese prints, studied with Pissarro in Paris and travelled to London in 1870-1 as well as south to the Mediterranean and to Venice. His paintings were selling in the USA by the late 1880s and in France his reputation was established by a major exhibition with Rodin in 1889. He created the gardens and lily ponds at his home in Giverny which provided endless inspiration from 1883. There is a series of Monet's **Waterlilies** (1927) in the Orangerie (closed until 2005), works in the Marmottan (16th) and at the Musée d'Orsay.

Napoleon I (1769-1821) He is the best-known, most controversial Corsican in French history. Napoleon Bonaparte's meteoric military career led to his promotion to General of the Interior in 1795, and First Consul in 1799. Hugely ambitious, he proclaimed himself Emperor of the French in 1804, was crowned in Notre-Dame by the Pope and assumed the title King of Italy the following year. As Emperor Napoleon I (1804-15) he created a dynasty, undertook the reorganization of Revolutionary France by introducing a Civil Code, and endowed Paris with monuments. He divorced Josephine de Beauharnais in 1809 and married Marie-Louise of Austria in 1810. Military successes were followed by humiliating losses. Allies became enemies. In 1809 he was at his peak but, having suffered defeat at the naval Battle of Trafalgar (1805), subjected France to a heavy toll during war with Spain (1808-14), experienced a humiliating withdrawal from Russia in 1812 and the surrender of Paris to the Prussians and Austrians in 1813, he was forced to abdicate in 1814. He returned in 1815 but was beaten by the English at Waterloo and abdicated a second time, ending his days on the island of St Helena. Among his great contributions to French culture was the reestablishment of the University of Paris in 1806. More transitory, but important influences on art in France at the time, were the paintings he commandeered from Italy. In the Louvre are paintings by David and Baron Gros of the Emperor and, most representative of monuments glorifying the Armies of the Republic and Empire, is the Carrousel Arch by the Napoleon's favourite architects Percier and Fontaine. His remains lie in the Dome des Invalides.

Napoleon III (1808-73) Louis Napoleon, Bonaparte's nephew, was elected Emperor Napoleon III in 1852. Major events during the Second Empire were a succession of wars, but also a policy of public works to clean up the cholera infected slums of medieval Paris. In place of tortuous lanes, which harboured insurrectionists, great boulevards were constructed (by Baron Haussmann), social housing was introduced, and train stations and covered markets were erected using the new metal framework technology. Napoleon III was responsible for transforming the Bois de Boulogne and Bois de Vincennes into public parks. Emblematic of the era is Garnier's Opera house (begun 1861), and the Napoleon III Apartments at the Louvre typify the grandiose interiors of the time. He was deposed and exiled in 1870 and, with his wife Eugénie, ended his days in England.

Neoclassical This term is applied to a theory of architecture which developed after the discovery of the ancient architectural treatise of Vitruvius in 1414. Architecture in the 17c used a classical language which derived from ancient Greece and Rome, and is identified by the harmonious relationship of the parts to the whole and the use of elements such as columns and pediments. A fine example of Neoclassical architecture in Paris is the Panthéon.

Nouvel, Jean (b. 1945) The hot name in French architecture, Nouvel is currently involved in the new Musée Branly, President Chirac's project for African, Asian, Oceanic and American arts. Nouvel hit the headlines with the striking Institut du Monde Arabe which opened in 1987. Among the Arabic references in the building, arranged around an interior court or *ryad* and a book tower or ziggourat, is the innovatively screened south wall with unique window shutters (*moucharabiehs*) which operate like a camera lens.

Pei, Ieoh Ming (b. 1917) The Chinese-born American architect who, with his associates, played a major role in the Grand Projet du Louvre which began in 1983. His most controversial vision was the design of the glazed Pyramid to serve as the new entrance to the museum; he and his team also created the remarkable new, lucid spaces in the Richelieu wing.

Perrault, Dominique (b. 1953) Perrault is the author of arguably the most megalomaniac but not the best thought through of the previous President's projects, the Bibliothèque Nationale de France, François-Mitterand, which opened in 1998. Four 79m-high towers shaped like open books stand on the corners of a wooden-decked esplanade, the centre of which is hollowed out to contain a garden. The reading rooms occupy the two levels around the garden-court.

Picasso, Pablo (1881-1973) The brilliant Spaniard became one of the most dominant personalities of the 20c in the visual arts. He was an extraordinarily prolific artist who collected ideas which he reinterpreted in a totally unique way. He settled in Paris in 1904 and from his Blue and Pink Periods he moved on to create works influenced by African art which led to *Les Demoiselles d'Avignon* (1907, New York) a turning point in his art. Together with Georges Braque he developed a new pictorial form which became known as Cubism. He practised a Neoclassical style between the wars, and then absorbed Surrealism whose re-interpretation is described as his Metamorphic phase. Collectors such as the American Gertrude Stein and Russian Sergei Shchukin began to buy his work by 1905. His most political work was *Guernica* (1937, Madrid) painted in reply to the horrors of the Spanish Civil War. His personal life was as varied as his professional one. He married the dancer Olga Koklova in 1918, and Jacqueline Roque in 1961, and his several other long-term lovers deeply influenced his work. He exercised a huge influence on modern art. As well as the Musée Picasso, there are examples of his work at the Centre Pompidou.

Poussin, Nicolas (c 1594-1665) He was the greatest of French classical painters and the Louvre owns a large number of his works but Poussin, who was born in Normandy, spent most of his life in Rome. He was exceedingly successful in producing small works for the bourgeois élite, predominantly of mythological subjects. His carefully balanced figures probably owe their rather rigid poses to his use of a three-dimensional visual aid in the shape of a small stage with wax models.

Renaissance Meaning rebirth or renewal, Humanist ideas of the Renaissance sprang from a reinterpretation of the values and culture of ancient Rome in Italy c 1420 and spread to all areas of creativity. Humanism placed a greater responsibility on the individual rather than on God as in the preceding Gothic period. Nature and philosophy also played an important role. Architecture was related more closely to the human scale, and painting synthesized Christianity, mythology and the every day. The first signs of the Renaissance in France were, however, decorative motifs introduced into architecture in the 16c and greater realism in painting. French Renaissance architecture developed its own particular national characteristics and was applied mainly to domestic architecture. The High Renaissance (c 1500-27) in art was a moment of intense harmony and control, combined with deep emotion and truth to nature. The Louvre is rich in Renaissance paintings of all periods from France, Italy and Northern Europe.

Rococo This applies mainly to a light, curvy and playful decoration used in France during the 18c, distinct from heavyweight Baroque. The name originates from *rocaille* or shell-like forms. The style spread throughout interior décor and occasionally to the exterior of buildings in the 18c.

Rodin, Auguste (1840-1917) One of the most celebrated sculptors of the late 19c. He started out as a stone mason and in 1877 began to be noticed for his work, *The Age of Bronze*. Michelangelo was a formative influence and in 1875 he went to Italy. His *Gates of Hell*, commissioned in 1880 for a new museum (never built), were only completed in 1917. Rodin had a profound influence on 20c sculpture although several artists (Maillot, Brancusi) made a deliberate effort to escape his spell: see Musée Rodin and Musée d'Orsay.

Rogers, Richard (b. 1933) and **Piano, Renzo** (b. 1937) The Italio-British team responsible for the eye-catching blend of high-tech tubes and sheet metal of the Pompidou Centre. It is named after its patron, President George Pompidou and was inaugurated in 1977. The Centre, with its functional elements (main escalator, air-conditioning) on the exterior picked out in primary colours, is, to say the least, a striking building. Heavily criticized in the past, it is now as much a part of the Right Bank as the Eiffel Tower is of the Left. A victim of its own success, the Centre attracted such huge crowds that it had to undergo a major overhaul in 1995-2000 in which Piano was heavily involved.

Saint Laurent, Yves (b. 1936) A name that conjures up Parisian chic was the great great grandson of the lawyer who drew up the wedding contract between Napoleon and Josephine. After winning a prize in a fashion competition, Saint Laurent moved to Paris in 1954 and was immediately taken on by Christian Dior. When Dior died in 1957, Saint Laurent succeeded him as the youngest ever couturier, setting up his own couture house in 1965. He is best known for the Trapeze line, the female tuxedo, and the trouser suit for women. In 1993 he sold his fashion house, and following a donation of £1 million to London's National Gallery, London, the wing for French painting is named after him. The last ever franc pieces to be minted carried his portrait.

Salon Members of the Academy held their exhibitions in the Salon d'Apollon in the Louvre from the 17c onwards. The Salon is still an annual event. During the 19c it became known as a rather stuffy and reactionary establishment against which the Impressionist and other avant-garde painters, having been rejected, put up a fight. They created alternative salons including the one-off Salon des Refusés in 1863. This was followed by the Salons d'Automne and des Indépendants which have both survived.

Surrealism A movement of the 1920-30s which penetrated the collective unconscious and rocked the visual arts. It developed from Dada, and was led by the writer André Breton (1896-1966) who took the word *surréaliste* from the poet Apollinaire's sub-title, *'un drame surréaliste'* of his farce *Les Mamelles de Tirésias* (1917). Breton defined the movement as 'pure psychic automatism' and drew up the First Surrealist Manifesto in 1924. The movement encompassed all the arts as well as politics, and set out to break down the contradictions between the conscious and unconscious. It drew inspiration from the writings of Sigmund Freud, dreams, found objects and their illogical juxtaposition. Ernst, Miró, Tanguy, Magritte, Duchamp and Dalí are among the best known Surrealist painters and the Centre Pompidou has many examples of their work.

Symbolism More a literary than a visual movement of the late 19c, possibly starting with Baudelaire's poem *Les Fleurs du Mal* (1857), it spread into painting. Artists most closely associated with Symbolism include Puvis de Chavannes (1824-98), Gustav Moreau (1826-98), Odilon Redon (1840-1916), as well as Gauguin and the Pont-Aven Group in Brittany. The best examples are at the Musée d'Orsay.

Toulouse-Lautrec, Henri de (1864-1901) Born into one of the most aristocratic families in France, Henri left southwest France to develop his artistic skills in Paris. By 1885 he had a studio in Montmartre and had absorbed the various trends of the avant-garde art world. He concentrated on the night life of Paris, including dance halls and prostitutes in *maisons closes*, which titillated the general public but which were often compassionate, satirical or objective studies. Lautrec's greatest breakthrough was thanks to lithography (introduced in 1798) which was an ideal technique for producing multiple copies of large posters and adapted well to his designs. Although he produced only 32 large posters, it is on these that his reputation stands.

Watteau, Antoine (1684-1721) Watteau painted compositions to enchant and divert. He arrived in Paris from Flanders c 1702 and stayed for most of his life. He started out painting theatrical scenes, and then decorative schemes including work for the Luxembourg Palace where he was exposed to the Rubens' Marie de Medici cycle. He also studied the Venetian painters. These influences came together in *Pilgrimage to Cythera* (1717, Louvre), typical of a type of hedonistic summer activity for which the term *fête galante* was invented. His paintings such as *Gilles* also have a disturbing air of melancholy. Because technically he was careless, his paintings have not aged well.

First edition 2004

Published by A&C Black Publishers Ltd
37 Soho Square, London W1D 3QZ

ISBN 0-7136-6696-X

Published in the United States of America by
WW Norton & Company, Inc
500 Fifth Avenue, New York, NY 10110, USA

ISBN 0-393-32595-4

Published simultaneously in Canada by
Penguin Books Canada Limited
10 Alcorn Avenue, Toronto, Ontario M4V 3BE

Series devised by Gemma Davies
Series designed by Jocelyn Lucas
Editorial and production: Gemma Davies, Jocelyn Lucas, Lilla Nwenu-Msimang, Miranda Robson, Kim Teo, Judy Tither

Maps by Mapping Company Ltd

Photographic acknowledgements
Front and inside front cover: *Still Life with Apples and Oranges* (detail on front cover) by Paul Cézanne, Musée d'Orsay, Paris © Photo: akg-images/ Erich Lessing. **Back cover image**: © Delia Gray-Durant.
Insides: Office de Tourisme de Paris: pp 6, 53, 171 by David Lefranc; p 61 by Fabian Charaffi; pp 39, 80, 83, 90, 103, 111, 131 by Catherine Balet.
Musée National du Moyen Age: p 97 © Farida Bzéchemier; p 98 © R.M.N.; p 99 © P. Painlevé/R.M.N.; p 100 © R.M.N.
Musée d'Orsay: p 117 © Sophie Boegly, Musée d'Orsay.
Musée Rodin: p 129 Jérôme Manoukian, © Musée Rodin; p 132 Béatrice Hatala, © Musée Rodin.
AKG-images: pp 15, 67 © Photo: akg-images; p 124 © Photo: akg-images/Erich Lessing.

Printed and bound in Singapore by Tien Wah Press (Pte.) Ltd

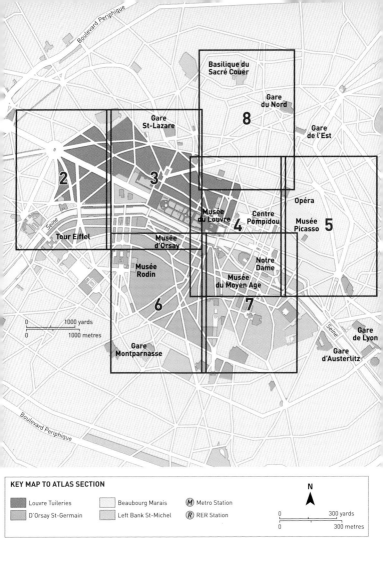

KEY MAP TO ATLAS SECTION

Louvre Tuileries

D'Orsay St-Germain

Beaubourg Marais

Left Bank St-Michel

Ⓜ Metro Station

Ⓡ RER Station

N

0   300 yards

0   300 metres

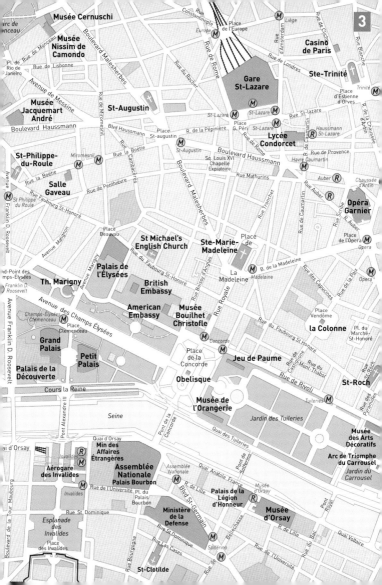